# BECOMING WHOLE

*Vulnerability, Brotherhood, And Joyful Masculinity*
*(Part 3 of the Unheld Series)*

**Gerald E. O.**

# Table of Contents

Table of Contents ................................................................... 2
A Note to the Reader ............................................................. 8
Why This Journal Exists ........................................................ 9
How to Use This Journal ..................................................... 10
What It Means to Be "Unheld" ........................................... 12
Daily Reflection Structure .................................................. 13
Day 230: Creating Brotherhood .......................................... 14
Day 231: Restoring the Circle ............................................. 19
Week 34: Expressing Without Fixing .................................. 23
Day 232: I Don't Have to Fix This ...................................... 23
Day 233: The Pressure to Be Useful ................................... 28
Day 234: Emotions Aren't Problems .................................. 32
Day 235: You Don't Need the Right Words ....................... 36
Day 236: No One Asked You to Be a Hero ........................ 40
Day 237: The Power of "Tell Me More" ............................ 44
Day 238: Let It Exist ........................................................... 48
Week 35: Masculinity Without Control .............................. 52
Day 239: Releasing the Reins ............................................. 52
Day 240: I Am Not the Fixer .............................................. 56
Day 241: The Masculine Pause ........................................... 60
Day 242: Vulnerability Without Fear ................................. 64
Day 243: Grounded, Not Guarded ...................................... 68
Day 244: Control Is a Story ................................................ 71
Month 8 Reflection: Mental Inventory ............................... 75
Day 245: The Power of Surrender ...................................... 75
Week 36: The Relationship Between Words & Wounds ... 79
Day 246: The First Wound ................................................. 79

Day 247: What Wasn't Said ............................................................... 84
Day 248: Words I've Weaponized ...................................................... 88
Day 249: Reclaiming Language ......................................................... 93
Day 250: The Words I Deserve .......................................................... 98
Day 251: Communicating My Truth ................................................ 102
Day 252: Healing Through Language ............................................. 106
WEEK 37: "Showing Up as Yourself — Fully" ................................ 110
DAY 253 — The Man in the Mirror ................................................ 110
DAY 254 — No More Small Talk with Myself ................................ 115
DAY 255 — Enough Without Earning ............................................ 119
DAY 256 — Living Without the Filter ............................................ 123
DAY 257 — Reclaiming My Voice ................................................... 127
DAY 258 — Holding Space for Myself ............................................ 131
DAY 259 — Fully Seen, Fully Me ..................................................... 135
WEEK 38: "The New ........................................................................ 139
DAY 260 — Redefining Freedom .................................................... 139
DAY 261 — Choosing Me Without Guilt ....................................... 143
DAY 262 — Free From Old Narratives ........................................... 147
DAY 264 — Saying No is Saying Yes ............................................... 155
DAY 265 — I Don't Owe My Pain to Anyone ................................ 159
DAY 266 — Free to Begin Again ..................................................... 163
WEEK 39 — Reclaiming Joy ............................................................. 167
DAY 267 — I Am Allowed to Enjoy My Life .................................. 167
DAY 268 — Joy After Pain ................................................................ 172
DAY 269 — Joy in the Ordinary ...................................................... 176
DAY 270 — Play Without Performance ......................................... 180
DAY 271 — Laughter is Liberation ................................................. 184
DAY 272 — You Deserve to Celebrate ............................................ 188
DAY 273 — Joy Is Also Masculine ................................................... 192
Month 9 Reflection: Restoration .................................................... 196

WEEK 40 — Building an Emotional Legacy ..................................... 197
DAY 274 — Legacy Isn't Just Material ........................................... 197
DAY 275: The Power of Emotional Inheritance ............................ 202
DAY 276 — Living as an Example .................................................. 206
DAY 277 — How You Make Others Feel ...................................... 210
DAY 278 — The Love You Leave Behind ..................................... 214
DAY 279 — Legacy in Small Moments ......................................... 218
DAY 280 — Becoming the Man You Needed ................................ 222
WEEK 41 — The Currency of Your Presence ................................ 226
DAY 281 — Presence Is Generosity ............................................... 226
DAY 282 — Distracted or Devoted? ............................................... 231
DAY 283 — Presence with Self ...................................................... 234
DAY 284 — Eye Contact and Heart Contact .................................. 238
DAY 285 — Being Where Your Feet Are ...................................... 242
DAY 286 — Holding Space ............................................................ 246
DAY 287 — The Quality of Presence ............................................. 251
WEEK 42 — The Version of Me I'm Becoming ............................ 256
DAY 288 — Becoming on Purpose ................................................ 256
DAY 289 — Meeting Future Me .................................................... 261
DAY 290 — Old Scripts, New Chapters ........................................ 266
DAY 291: Becoming Doesn't Require Burning ............................. 270
DAY 292 — A New Definition of Strength ................................... 274
DAY 293 — The Inner Compass .................................................... 279
DAY 294 — Becoming Whole, Not Perfect .................................. 283
WEEK 43 — ................................................................................... 287
The Unwritten Letter ..................................................................... 287
DAY 295 — If I Could Speak Freely ............................................. 287
DAY 296 — The Letter I Never Sent ............................................. 292
DAY 297 — An Apology to Myself ............................................... 297
DAY 298 — What I Wish I'd Heard .............................................. 302

DAY 299: Dear Younger Me .............................................................307
DAY 300: Letters Left Unread .........................................................312
DAY 301: The Letter I'll Live By .....................................................317
WEEK 44 — Returning Home to Myself ...........................................322
DAY 302 : The Man I Am ..............................................................322
DAY 304:  Safe Inside My Skin ......................................................332
Month 10 Reflection: Gratitude + Grief ...........................................337
DAY 305 — Reclaiming My Narrative ............................................337
DAY 306 — Living Without Permission .........................................343
DAY 307: My Peace, My Priority ...................................................348
DAY 308: Home Is Me .................................................................353
WEEK 45 — Love, .......................................................................358
DAY 309: Letting Love In .............................................................358
DAY 310: Love Without Armor .....................................................363
DAY 311:  I Am Lovable ...............................................................368
DAY 312: Love Is Not a Transaction ...............................................373
DAY 313 — Loving From Overflow ...............................................377
DAY 315: Love Starts Here ...........................................................384
WEEK 46 — Spiritual Integrity ......................................................389
DAY 316: What Do I Believe? .......................................................389
DAY 317: When Belief Becomes Behavior .....................................395
DAY 318: Sacred, Not Spectacle ....................................................399
DAY 319: Your Life Is Your Message .............................................403
DAY 320: Don't Weaponize Your Wisdom .....................................408
DAY 321: Permission to Evolve .....................................................412
DAY 322: The Integrity of Rest ......................................................417
WEEK 47 — Joyful Masculinity .....................................................422
DAY 323: Permission to Be Soft ....................................................422
DAY 324: Redefining Strength ......................................................427
DAY 325: The Joy of Brotherhood .................................................432

DAY 326: Play Is Power ..........437
DAY 327: The Masculine Body ..........441
DAY 328: Celebration Is Sacred ..........445
DAY 329 : I Am Enough ..........450
WEEK 48 — Fathers, Fatherhood & Forgiveness ..........455
DAY 330: The Father I Needed ..........455
DAY 331: Naming the Hurt ..........460
DAY 332: Forgiveness Is for Me ..........464
DAY 333: Becoming the Father ..........468
DAY 334: Healing the Bloodline ..........472
DAY 335: If I Could Say One Thing ..........476
Month 11 Reflection: Refinement ..........480
DAY 336: I Am Not My Father ..........480
WEEK 49 — Loved, ..........485
Received ..........485
DAY 337: The Courage to Receive ..........485
DAY 338: Lowering the Armor ..........490
DAY 339: Letting Love Find Me ..........495
DAY 340: Love From Within ..........499
DAY 341: Safe to Be Loved ..........504
DAY 342: Love in Action ..........509
DAY 343: I Let It In ..........513
Week 50: The Power of Presence ..........518
Day 344: The Gift of Now ..........518
Day 345: Here, Not Elsewhere ..........522
Day 346: When You Truly Listen ..........526
Day 347: Discomfort Is a Doorway ..........530
Day 348: Being, Not Doing ..........534
Day 349: Fully Alive ..........538
Day 350: Stay with Yourself ..........543

Week 51: Holding Peace in the Chaos ............................................. 547
Day 351: Calm Is a Choice ............................................................. 547
Day 352: Letting It Be .................................................................... 552
Day 353: Grounded, Not Reactive .................................................. 557
Day 354: The Safe Place Within .................................................... 562
Day 355: Choose Not to Escalate ................................................... 567
Day 356: Stillness Is Strength ........................................................ 571
Day 357: Harmony Over Hustle ..................................................... 575
Week 52: Becoming Whole ............................................................ 579
Day 358: The Man I Am Now ........................................................ 579
Day 359: Lessons That Remain ...................................................... 584
Day 360: Wholeness Over Perfection ............................................. 588
Day 361: Holding the Mirror .......................................................... 592
Day 362: It Was Always Within You ............................................. 597
Day 363: Preparing to Begin Again ................................................ 602
Day 364: A Letter to the Future Me ............................................... 607
Day 365: UNHELD, UNBROKEN ................................................ 611
Month 12 Reflection: Arrival & Becoming .................................... 617
Resources for Men's Mental Health & Mindful Living .................. 618
    Mental Health & Therapy for Men ............................................ 618
    Mindfulness & Meditation Tools ............................................... 619
    Support Networks for Men ........................................................ 619
Closing Note: The Journey Continues ............................................ 621
Acknowledgements ........................................................................ 622

# A Note to the Reader

This is not your typical journal.

This isn't about "fixing" you, improving your productivity, or turning you into some hyper-masculine ideal. This is a journal for the man who has carried too much, said too little, and felt unseen in the process. It's for the man who performs strength so well, no one notices when he's breaking inside.

Maybe that man is you.

UNHELD is a safe place — not to be perfect, but to be *present*. It's here to remind you that you are allowed to feel, to unravel, to be unsure, to rest, to breathe. You are allowed to want softness. You are allowed to want more.

Each page of this journal was written with you in mind. Not the version of you that holds it together for everyone else
— but the one underneath. The one who aches for peace. The one who just wants to be heard.

You're not alone here. Welcome home to yourself.

# Why This Journal Exists

For generations, men have been taught to hold it in.

We've inherited silences. We've worn masks so long they feel like skin. We've confused numbness for strength, isolation for pride, and exhaustion for worth. Somewhere along the way, we lost access to our full humanity — and with it, the tools to heal. This journal was born from that ache.

UNHELD exists because men deserve a space to feel without judgment. To explore their minds and emotions without the burden of performance. To practice mindfulness in a way that is both powerful and practical. To unlearn, reframe, and reconnect.

It exists because silence is no longer sustainable — and your wholeness matters.

# How to Use This Journal

You'll find **365 days** of intentional reflection — one for each day of your year. You can begin in January or July, on your birthday or after a breakdown. There's no wrong time to start showing up for yourself.

Each daily page includes:

A *Mindful Insight* to challenge, ground, or inspire you. A *Prompt* to guide your reflection.

A *Mindful Minute* to pause and breathe.

An *Unheld Moment* — a truth, observation, or tension you may relate to.

Space to *journal freely* — for your thoughts, emotions, questions, or prayers.

At the end of each month, you'll find a **Monthly Reflection Page** to track your emotional growth, celebrate the unseen, and center your next steps.

You'll also have special pages for:

*Letters You Never Sent* — things you've always wanted to say.

*Your Emotional Toolbox* — practical coping tools and grounding techniques.

**Daily Mantras** — powerful affirmations for presence, softness, and strength.

**Dreams, Goals & Visions** — a space to imagine with no deadlines.

**Coloring & Release Pages** — spaces for creative expression and emotional release.

Use this journal daily, weekly, or whenever you need it. Let it be what it needs to be — some days a mirror, some days a friend.

# What It Means to Be "Unheld"

To be **unheld** is to be strong in public and shattered in private.
It's the feeling of being praised for resilience no one helped
you build.
It's knowing how to support others but not how to ask for
support.
It's being so used to surviving, you forget what living feels
like.

But this journal reclaims the word.

To be *unheld* here is not a flaw — it's a beginning. It's the quiet truth that healing is overdue.
It's a man deciding that numbness is not his legacy.

This is not the end of you holding it together.
It's the beginning of you holding *yourself* — with grace.

# Daily Reflection Structure

Every daily page in this journal is intentionally structured to support mindful masculinity — a balance of awareness, softness, and strength. Here's what to expect each day:

- Mindful Insight
  A daily observation, principle, or invitation rooted in mindfulness and emotional awareness.
- Reflection Prompt
  A thought-provoking question or prompt that encourages you to go inward and speak your truth.
- Mindful Minute
  A quick grounding practice — breathwork, stillness, gratitude, or presence. One minute is enough.
- Unheld Moment
  A relatable tension, truth, or struggle men carry but rarely name. You're not alone in this.
- Daily Journaling Space
  Blank space to write. No rules. Use it to vent, affirm, question, dream, or simply *be*.
- Quarterly Progress Markers
  At every 3-month interval, you'll pause for a deeper reflection — to honor your journey so far, reset your focus, and track your emotional evolution.

# Day 230: Creating Brotherhood

Brotherhood isn't always inherited.
Sometimes, it's built—
in honest conversations,
in showing up again and again,
in letting another man know
he doesn't have to do it all alone.

It's born when silence is broken,
when shoulders carry shared stories,
when presence says, *"You matter."*

Brotherhood is not just connection.
It's safety.
It's witnessing.
It's choosing each other, on purpose.

**Reflection:**

- What stops you from forming deeper connections with other men?

_____
_____
_____
_____
_____
_____
_____

**Prompt:**

- Brainstorm small ways you could initiate or deepen male friendships — today or this week.

_____
_____
_____
_____
_____
_____
_____

**Mindful Minute:**

- As you breathe, imagine planting a seed. Each breath is care. Friendship grows with patience.

_____
_____
_____
_____
_____
_____
_____

## Mantra:

*"I can initiate the connection I crave."*

## Evening Reflection:

- **Did you take a step toward connection today?**

_____
_____
_____
_____
_____
_____
_____

# Day 231: Restoring the Circle

Somewhere along the way,
the circle of men fractured—
competition replacing connection,
silence replacing support.

But the circle can be restored.
When men gather with softness,
with truth,
with open hands instead of closed fists—
something sacred returns.

A remembering.
A healing.
A brotherhood that doesn't require armor.
Only presence.

**Morning Reflection:**

- Imagine a circle of men where everyone is honest, supported, and safe. What does that space feel like?

_____
_____
_____
_____
_____
_____
_____

**Prompt:**

- What would it take for you to build or find that kind of circle in your life?

_____
_____
_____
_____
_____
_____
_____

### Mindful Minute:

With each breath, whisper: "I belong." Feel it as truth.

### Mantra:

*"Brotherhood begins with me."*

### Evening Reflection:

- **Do you feel more open to community now than you did a week ago?**

_____
_____
_____
_____
_____
_____
_____

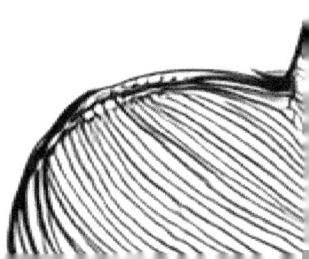

# Week 34: Expressing Without Fixing

Men are often taught to fix — problems, people, themselves. But not every emotion or moment needs solving. This week is about allowing feelings to be felt and expressed, without rushing to repair or suppress them. True presence is enough.

# Day 232: I Don't Have to Fix This

Not every wound needs a solution.
Not every silence needs to be filled.

Sometimes, the most loving thing I can do
is to stay — open, present, and quiet.
To bear witness, not to solve.
To hold space, not to control.

I'm learning that comfort doesn't always come
from fixing the pain,
but from not facing it alone.

**Morning Reflection:**

- When someone shares their pain with you, do you feel pressure to solve it?

_____
_____
_____
_____
_____
_____
_____

**Prompt:**

- Write about a moment when you wished you could help but didn't know how.

_____
_____
_____
_____
_____
_____
_____

- **What might have happened if you had just listened?**

_____
_____
_____
_____
_____
_____
_____

**Mindful Minute:**

Take three deep breaths. Say: *"I offer presence, not solutions."*

**Mantra:**

*"Witnessing is powerful."*

**Evening Reflection:**

- **Were you able to simply listen today?**

_____
_____
_____
_____
_____
_____
_____

- **How did that feel?**

_____
_____
_____
_____
_____
_____
_____

# Day 233: The Pressure to Be Useful

Somewhere along the way, I confused love with usefulness.
As if my value lived only in what I could give, do, or solve.

But I am not a tool.
I am a person.

Even when I'm still, unproductive, or simply present—
I am worthy.
Not because I'm useful,
but because I exist.

**Morning Reflection:**

- **Do you ever feel that your worth is tied to what you do, not who you are?**

_____
_____
_____
_____
_____
_____
_____

**Prompt:**

- **Where did this belief come from, and how is it affecting your relationships?**

_____
_____
_____
_____
_____
_____
_____
_____

**Mindful Minute:**

Place your hand on your chest. Breathe into your being — not your doing.

**Mantra:**

*"I am worthy without being useful."*

**Evening Reflection:**

- What did you offer today simply by being present?

_____
_____
_____
_____
_____
_____
_____

# Day 234: Emotions Aren't Problems

I used to treat emotions like problems to be solved.
As if sadness needed fixing.
As if anger made me broken.
As if fear meant failure.

But emotions aren't emergencies.
They're messengers.

Now, I listen—without rushing to silence them.
I sit with what comes.
Because feeling isn't failure.
It's being human.

**Morning Reflection:**

- Which emotions do you try to avoid, ignore, or silence?

_____
_____
_____
_____
_____
_____
_____

**Prompt:**

- **Choose one "uncomfortable" emotion and write it a letter. Let it speak.**

_____
_____
_____
_____
_____
_____
_____
_____

### Mindful Minute:

Feel the emotion you chose. Don't analyze — just notice.

### Mantra:

*"Feeling is healing."*

**Evening Reflection:**

- What shifted when you let the emotion exist?

_____
_____
_____
_____
_____
_____
_____
_____

# Day 235: You Don't Need the Right Words

Sometimes, there are no perfect words.
No tidy phrases to hold the weight of what we feel.

But presence speaks.
Silence can cradle.
A hand on the shoulder, a nod, a pause—
they say more than polished sentences ever could.

You don't need the right words.
You just need to be real.
That is enough.

**Morning Reflection:**

- **Have you ever held back from comforting someone because you didn't know what to say?**

_____
_____
_____
_____
_____
_____
_____

**Prompt:**

- **Write about a time someone's quiet presence helped you more than words ever could.**

_____
_____
_____
_____
_____
_____
_____
_____

### Mindful Minute:

Inhale for four, exhale for six. Let silence settle inside.

### Mantra:

*"Presence speaks louder than perfection."*

**Evening Reflection:**

■ Were you able to sit in silence with someone (or yourself) today?

_____
_____
_____
_____
_____
_____
_____
_____

# Day 236: No One Asked You to Be a Hero

**Morning Reflection:**

- Do you take on others' pain as your own responsibility?

_____
_____
_____
_____
_____
_____
_____
_____

**Prompt:**

- Who are you trying to rescue, and what are you hoping to prove?

_____
_____
_____
_____
_____

_____
_____
_____

### Mindful Minute:

Repeat to yourself gently: *"I am not responsible for everyone's healing."*

### Mantra:

*"I support without saving."*

**Evening Reflection:**

- **How did you release the need to fix today?**

_____
_____
_____
_____
_____
_____
_____

# Day 237: The Power of "Tell Me More"

Not every moment calls for advice.
Sometimes, it just asks for space—
an invitation to unfold.

"Tell me more" is a soft door,
one that lets another step into their truth
without fear of correction or fixing.

It says:
I'm here.
I care.
I'm listening.

Morning Reflection:

- When was the last time you truly invited someone to open up without judgment?

_____
_____
_____
_____
_____
_____
_____

Prompt:

- Write about a conversation where you wish you had listened more. How would you show up differently now?

_____
_____
_____
_____
_____
_____
_____

### Mindful Minute:

Close your eyes and repeat: *"I create space for truth."*

### Mantra:

*"Curiosity is connection."*

### Evening Reflection:

Did you offer space for truth today? How did it feel?

# Day 238: Let It Exist

Not every feeling needs a solution.
Not every ache needs a name.
Some things simply need permission—
to breathe, to unfold, to be.

Let it exist.
Without rushing it away.
Without demanding it explain itself.

Because presence is powerful.
And allowing is a form of love.

**Morning Reflection:**

- **What part of yourself are you still trying to "fix" before it deserves love?**

_____
_____
_____
_____
_____
_____
_____

**Prompt:**

- scribe that part with compassion, as if you were speaking to a friend.

_____
_____
_____
_____
_____
_____
_____
_____

**Mindful Minute:**

With each breath, whisper: *"Even this is worthy."*

**Mantra:**

*"I can hold without changing."*

**Evening Reflection:**

- What part of you felt seen today — without needing to be better?

_____
_____
_____
_____
_____
_____
_____

# Week 35: Masculinity Without Control

Masculinity isn't about domination, perfection, or emotional stoicism. This week explores a grounded masculinity—one that isn't dependent on control, but rooted in emotional clarity, presence, and truth. What if your power came from surrender, not force?

## Day 239: Releasing the Reins

Control feels like safety—
a way to protect what matters,
to manage what hurts.

But holding too tightly
can keep us from healing,
from receiving,
from resting.

Today, I loosen my grip.
Not out of weakness,
but out of trust—
that life can hold me, too.

**Morning Reflection:**

- What do you fear would happen if you let go of control?

_____
_____
_____
_____
_____
_____
_____

**Prompt:**

- Describe an area of life where you're gripping too tightly. What would loosening your grip look like?

_____
_____
_____
_____
_____
_____
_____

**Mindful Minute:**

As you **inhale**, whisper *"I release…"* — as you **exhale**, say *"…the need to control."*

**Mantra:**

*"Letting go is strength."*

**Evening Reflection:**

- **Did you surrender something today? How did that feel in your body?**

_____
_____
_____
_____
_____
_____
_____

# Day 240: I Am Not the Fixer

I've carried the weight of everyone's storms,
believing love meant solving,
believing peace meant mending.

But I am not the fixer.
I am a witness,
a presence,
a soft place to land.

It is not mine to rescue —
only to remain.

**Morning Reflection:**

- Do you feel pressure to solve every issue in your relationships?

_____
_____
_____
_____
_____
_____

**Prompt:**

- Write about a time when trying to fix something made things worse. What did you learn?

_____
_____
_____
_____
_____
_____
_____
_____

### Mindful Minute:

Place your palm on your chest. Say, *"It's okay not to have all the answers."*

### Mantra:

*"Support doesn't require control."*

**Evening Reflection:**

- What did you allow to unfold today without stepping in to solve?

_____
_____
_____
_____
_____
_____
_____

# Day 241: The Masculine Pause

There is power in the pause—
not in action, but in awareness.
Not in proving, but in presence.

The masculine pause is not withdrawal;
it is a return to center,
a breath between the doing,
where clarity finds us
and softness is not shameful.

It is here I remember:
I don't need to rush to matter.

**Morning Reflection:**

- **When was the last time you paused before reacting?**

_____
_____
_____
_____
_____
_____
_____

**Prompt:**

- **Reflect on a situation where your impulse was to act. What might have happened if you paused first?**

_____
_____
_____
_____
_____
_____
_____
_____

## Mindful Minute:

Breathe deeply and slowly count to ten. Feel each second fully.

## Mantra:

*"Stillness leads me."*

**Evening Reflection:**

- **How did pausing shift the energy of your day?**

_____
_____
_____
_____
_____
_____
_____
_____

# Day 242: Vulnerability Without Fear

To be vulnerable without fear
is not to be fearless—
but to be willing.

Willing to be seen,
to let the armor loosen,
to speak before the words are perfect,
to feel before the moment is safe.

In this space,
I make room for truth—
and call it strength.

**Morning Reflection:**

- **What's one truth about yourself you rarely share?**

_____
_____
_____
_____
_____
_____
_____

**Prompt:**

- Write the thing you're afraid to say out loud. Let it exist on the page.

_____
_____
_____
_____
_____
_____
_____
_____

### Mindful Minute:

Breathe into your throat and heart. Whisper, *"I am safe to speak truth."*

### Mantra:

*"My truth doesn't weaken me."*

**Evening Reflection:**

- **What truth did you get closer to today?**

_____
_____
_____
_____
_____
_____
_____
_____

# Day 243: Grounded, Not Guarded

There's a difference between being grounded and being guarded.
One is rooted. The other is closed.
One draws from presence. The other, from protection.

I no longer confuse stillness with silence,
or boundaries with walls.

I can stand firm
without shutting down.
I can be grounded—
and still let love in.

**Morning Reflection:**

- **Does your strength ever feel like a mask?**

_____
_____
_____
_____
_____
_____
_____

**Prompt:**

- **Explore the difference between being grounded and being guarded. Which do you rely on more?**

_____
_____
_____
_____
_____
_____
_____
_____

**Mindful Minute:**

Stand barefoot, if possible. Breathe and imagine roots from your feet deep into the earth.

**Mantra:**

*"I am rooted, not rigid."*

**Evening Reflection:**

- **When did you choose presence over protection today?**

_____
_____
_____
_____
_____
_____
_____

# Day 244: Control Is a Story

Control gave me comfort—
a script I could cling to
when everything else felt uncertain.

But control was just a story—
a fragile illusion
masquerading as safety.

Today, I choose presence over prediction.
Trust over tension.
Because life isn't a problem to solve,
but a mystery to meet.

**Morning Reflection:**

- **What stories do you tell yourself to feel in control?**

_____
_____
_____
_____
_____
_____
_____

**Prompt:**

- **Write one controlling narrative you've carried (e.g., "If I don't do it, it won't be done right"). How does it limit you?**

_____
_____
_____
_____
_____
_____
_____

### Mindful Minute:

Inhale clarity. Exhale fear. Repeat.

### Mantra:

*"Control is not connection."*

**Evening Reflection:**

- **What story did you challenge or rewrite today?**

_____
_____
_____
_____
_____
_____
_____
_____

# Month 8 Reflection: Mental Inventory

1. **What I've Learned About Myself This Month**

- **List a few things—patterns, truths, or surprises.**

# Day 245: The Power of Surrender

Surrender isn't giving up—
it's laying down the armor
I no longer need.

It's trusting the moment,
even when I don't understand it.
It's releasing control,
so I can finally rest in truth.

There is strength
in not forcing.
There is power
in letting go.

**Morning Reflection:**

- What's the difference between giving up and surrendering?

_____
_____
_____
_____
_____
_____
_____
_____

**Prompt:**

- Write about one thing you're ready to surrender—not because you're weak, but because you're wise.

_____
_____
_____
_____
_____
_____
_____
_____

### Mindful Minute:

Sit in silence. Release tension with each exhale. Let your hands fall open.

### Mantra:

*"Surrender is sacred."*

**Evening Reflection:**

- **How did surrender serve your peace today?**

_____
_____
_____
_____
_____
_____
_____

# Week 36: The Relationship Between Words & Wounds

Words shape our wounds—and sometimes, they are the wounds. What was said (or unsaid) to us in boyhood often echoes into adulthood. This week, we lean into the silence between sentences and begin to reframe our narratives.

## Day 246: The First Wound

Before I had words for pain,
I felt it.

Not always loud or violent—
sometimes just the ache
of not being held,
not being heard.

The first wound wasn't always
a moment.
Sometimes it was
a pattern.

But naming it now
isn't about blame.
It's about understanding
where I began—
so I can choose
how I heal.


**Morning Reflection:**

- **What's the first memory you have of being hurt by words?**

_____
_____
_____
_____
_____
_____
_____

**Prompt:**

- **Describe that moment. Who said what?**

_____
_____
_____
_____
_____
_____
_____
_____

- **How did it land in your heart?**

_____
_____
_____
_____
_____
_____
_____
_____

**Mindful Minute:**

Place your hand over your heart. Whisper to yourself: "I remember. I survived."

### Mantra:

*"I am healing what I once believed."*

### Evening Reflection:

- **How did today's reflection shift your understanding of your early pain?**

_____
_____
_____
_____
_____
_____
_____
_____

# Day 247: What Wasn't Said

Sometimes, silence speaks louder
than any word ever could.
What wasn't said
shaped me, too.

The apology that never came.
The "I'm proud of you"
that hung in the air,
waiting.

The missing reassurance.
The withheld tenderness.

But today, I make space
for those quiet absences.
Not to resent—
but to acknowledge
how deeply I needed them.

And how I'm learning
to say them now
—to myself,
and to others.

**Morning Reflection:**

- Sometimes silence speaks louder than any insult. What love did you need to hear but never did?

_____
_____
_____
_____
_____
_____
_____
_____

**Prompt:**

- Write a letter to your younger self, saying all the things you needed someone to say back then.

_____
_____
_____
_____
_____
_____
_____
_____

### Mindful Minute:

Close your eyes. Hear the words you wish were spoken. Let them land.

### Mantra:

*"I give myself the words I needed."*

### Evening Reflection:

- **What part of you softened after speaking to your younger self today?**

_____
_____
_____
_____
_____
_____
_____
_____

# Day 248: Words I've Weaponized

There are words I've used
not to heal,
but to shield.

Sarcasm as armor.
Critique as distance.
Silence as punishment.
Kindness, only when it felt safe.

I've turned language into a sword
when I felt small,
when I feared rejection,
when I didn't know how to ask
for closeness without control.

But I'm learning now
to put down the weapons—
to let my words build bridges,
not walls.

Gentle doesn't mean weak.
It means brave enough
to speak with care.

**Morning Reflection:**

- Have you ever used words to push someone away before they could hurt you?

_____
_____
_____
_____
_____
_____
_____
_____

**Prompt:**

- Write about a time you hurt someone with your words. What were you protecting?

_____
_____
_____
_____
_____
_____
_____
_____

**Mindful Minute:**

Breathe in accountability. Breathe out shame.

**Mantra:**

*"My growth includes owning my impact."*

**Evening Reflection:**

- What did you learn about your own emotional defenses today?

_____
_____
_____
_____
_____
_____
_____
_____

# Day 249: Reclaiming Language

There was a time
I used words to disappear—
to please, to perform,
to protect others from my truth.

I learned to twist my voice
into something palatable,
something small,
something safe for everyone but me.

But now, I reclaim my language.

I speak not to be accepted,
but to be honest.
Not to impress,
but to connect.
Not to hide,
but to heal.

My words belong to me.
And    I    am
allowed   to   use
them        fully.
Loudly.
Gently.
Truthfully.

**Morning Reflection:**

- **What labels or names were you called that still cling to your identity?**

_____
_____
_____
_____
_____
_____
_____
_____

**Prompt:**

Write those words down. Then rewrite them with truth and compassion.

_____
_____
_____
_____
_____
_____
_____
_____

**Mindful Minute:**

Gently tap your chest with your fingertips. Say: "I reclaim my name."

**Mantra:**

*"Only I define who I am."*

**Evening Reflection:**

- How did rewriting your identity feel in your body?

_____
_____
_____
_____
_____
_____
_____

# Day 250: The Words I Deserve

I grew up learning to swallow silence,
to settle for scraps of kindness,
to live on compliments laced with condition.

But I deserve better.

I deserve words that soothe,
not sharpen.
Words that lift,
not weigh down.
Words that see me clearly,
and still choose to stay.

I deserve to be spoken to with love—
by others, yes,
but especially by myself.

Today, I offer myself

Morning Reflection:

- What words do you long to hear from someone right now?

_____
_____
_____
_____
_____
_____
_____
_____

Prompt:

- Write a script where someone says those exact words to you—and believe it.

_____
_____
_____
_____
_____
_____
_____
_____
_____

### Mindful Minute:

Say the words aloud. Receive them.

### Mantra:

*"I am worthy of kind words."*

### Evening Reflection:

- **How did it feel to hear what you've been waiting for?**

_____
_____
_____
_____
_____
_____
_____
_____

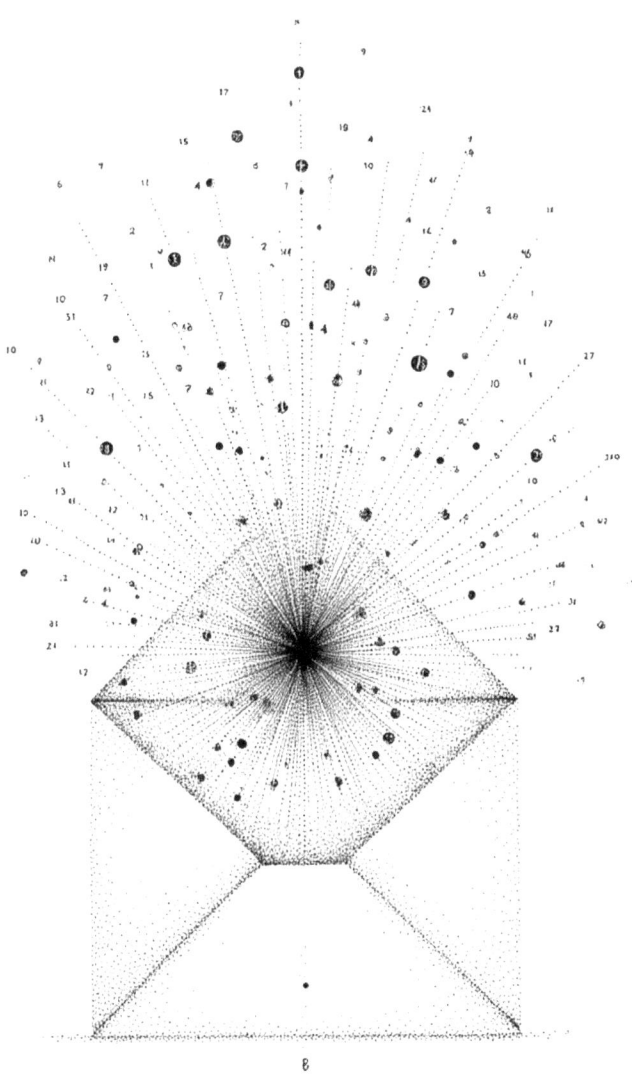

# Day 251: Communicating My Truth

For too long, I said what was safe.
What was expected.
What would keep the peace.

But silence has a cost.

Today, I honor my voice.
Not to argue. Not to impress.
But to live honestly.
To say what I mean—without apology.

My truth may not please everyone.
But it frees me.
It brings me closer to the life that fits,
not the one that simply functions.

My words are not weapons.
They are bridges.
They are boundaries.
They are home.

**Morning Reflection:**

- Do you say what you mean—or do you filter it to be safe or small?

_____
_____
_____
_____
_____
_____
_____

**Prompt:**

- Write about a truth you've been afraid to say. Then, imagine saying it with calm confidence.

_____
_____
_____
_____
_____
_____
_____

**Mindful Minute:**

Place one hand on your throat, the other on your stomach. Breathe deeply into both.

**Mantra:**

*"My truth matters."*

**Evening Reflection:**

- **Did you express something today you usually suppress?**

_____
_____
_____
_____
_____
_____
_____
_____

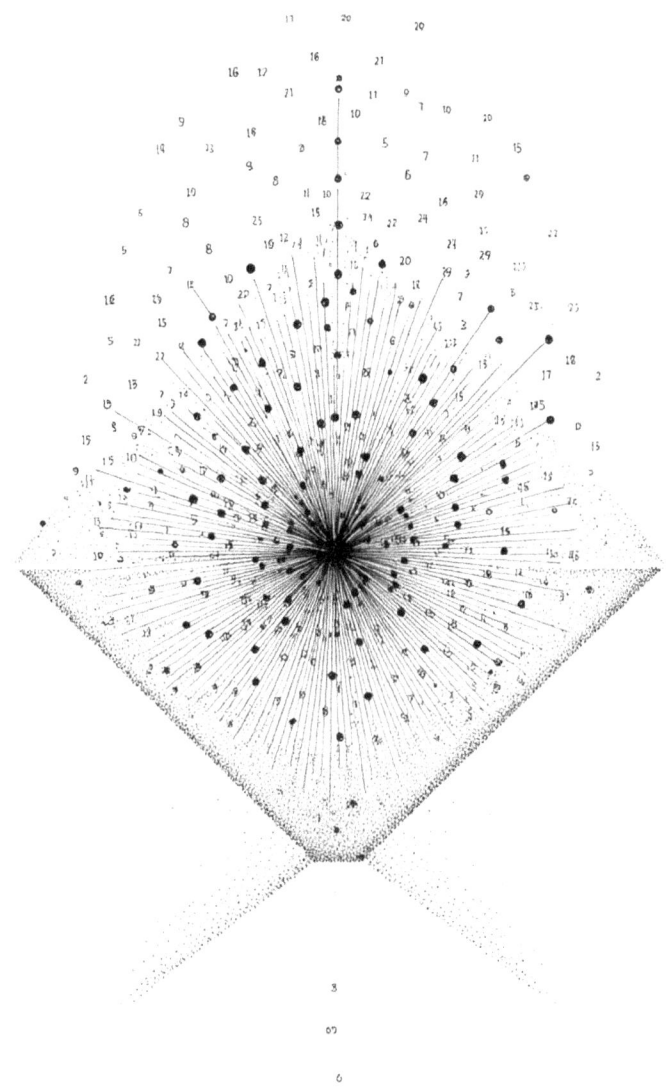

# Day 252: Healing Through Language

Words have harmed me.
But they can also heal me.

There was a time I didn't know how to name what I felt—
so I swallowed it.
Numbed it.
Let it twist into something heavier than truth.

But now, I speak gently to myself.
I say things I never heard growing up:
"You're allowed to feel."
"You are not too much."
"You matter."

Language can be medicine—
not because it fixes everything,
but because it allows me to be seen,
by others
and by myself.

I don't need perfect words.
Just honest ones.
Healing starts there.

**Morning Reflection:**

Can words heal what words once harmed?

**Prompt:**

- **Write a new story—a story where you speak your truth, are met with understanding, and feel whole.**

_____
_____
_____
_____
_____
_____
_____
_____
_____

**Mindful Minute:**

Breathe into possibility. Let hope settle.

### Mantra:

*"My story is evolving."*

### Evening Reflection:

- **What did this new story unlock in you today?**

_____
_____
_____
_____
_____
_____
_____
_____

# WEEK 37: "Showing Up as Yourself — Fully"

This week is about authenticity — the courageous act of removing the masks, softening the armor, and allowing yourself to be fully seen. Not the version of you that pleases, performs, or protects others, but the man you are at your core. That man is enough.

# DAY 253 — The Man in the Mirror

There were seasons I avoided him.
Not out of pride, but out of pain.
The man staring back felt unfamiliar—
too burdened, too tired, too unsure.

But the mirror doesn't lie.
It reflects not just the face,
but the fight behind the eyes.

And slowly, I've come to meet him again—
not with judgment, but with kindness.
Not with shame, but with presence.

He's not perfect.
But he's still here.
Still growing.
Still showing up.

And that is enough.

### Morning Reflection:

When I look in the mirror, do I see a reflection or a performance? Today, I challenge myself to meet my own eyes without judgment.

### Prompt:

- **What parts of yourself have you kept hidden?**

_____
_____
_____
_____
_____
_____
_____
_____

- Why?

_____
_____
_____
_____
_____
_____

**Mindful Minute:**

Breathe deeply. Gently press your hand to your chest.

Say out loud, "I see you."

### Mantra:

*I am not my performance. I am my presence.*

### Evening Reflection:

- **In what ways did I show up more honestly today?**

_____
_____
_____
_____
_____
_____
_____
_____

# DAY 254 — No More Small Talk with Myself

I've mastered polite deflection—
even in the silence of my own mind.
Asking safe questions.
Giving rehearsed answers.
Avoiding the depth that might shake something loose.

But I deserve honesty.

**Morning Reflection:**

I deserve real conversations — especially with myself.
Today, I choose honesty over comfort.

**Prompt:**

- What truths have you been avoiding in your self-talk?

_____
_____
_____
_____
_____
_____
_____

**Mindful Minute:**

Sit in silence. Ask, "What am I really feeling?" Let the answer come.

**Mantra:**

*Truth begins with me.*

**Evening Reflection:**

- **What did I learn about myself today that surprised me?**

_____
_____
_____
_____
_____
_____
_____
_____

# DAY 255 — Enough Without Earning

What if I didn't need to prove it?
What if my worth wasn't something to hustle for,
or achieve, or justify?

What if being here —
with breath in my lungs and a heart still learning —
was already enough?

Somewhere beneath the noise of striving,
there's a quieter truth:
I was never meant to earn love.
I was meant to receive it.

**Morning Reflection:**

I don't have to earn the right to rest, to feel, to be. I am already enough.

**Prompt:**

- Where in your life do you feel you're constantly "earning" your worth?

_____
_____
_____
_____
_____
_____
_____

**Mindful Minute:**

Place both feet firmly on the ground. Whisper, "I deserve peace."

**Mantra:**

*I was worthy before I proved anything.*

**Evening Reflection:**

- **Did I rest today without guilt?**

_____
_____
_____
_____
_____
_____
_____

- **Why or why not?**

_____
_____
_____
_____
_____
_____
_____
_____

# DAY 256 — Living Without the Filter

I've spent years editing myself —
shrinking the edges, softening the truth,
saying what's safe instead of what's real.

But filtering my voice
only made me feel further from myself.
More "acceptable," maybe.
But never truly seen.

Now I'm learning to speak unfiltered.
To let my truth stand without explanation.
To live as I am —
whole, honest, and unhidden.

**Morning Reflection:**

Life isn't meant to be lived through a filter. My truth, in all its forms, is beautiful.

**Prompt:**

- **When do you find yourself performing or filtering who you are?**

_____
_____
_____
_____
_____
_____
_____
_____

### Mindful Minute:

Stretch, unclench, exhale deeply. Practice softening your body and voice.

## Mantra:

*My unfiltered self is enough.*

## Evening Reflection:

- **Where did I let someone see the real me today?**

_____
_____
_____
_____
_____
_____
_____
_____

# DAY 257 — Reclaiming My Voice

There were times I swallowed my words
to keep the peace,
to avoid judgment,
to be what others needed.

But silence turned into self-betrayal.
And the longer I stayed quiet,
the more distant I felt from myself.

Now I'm learning to speak —
not to convince, not to perform,
but to connect.

Each word I claim
is a piece of myself I return to.
My voice is not too much.
It's mine — and it matters.

**Morning Reflection:**

Silence isn't always strength. Today, I reclaim the right to speak — softly, honestly, freely.

**Prompt:**

- **What have you not said out loud that needs to be heard?**

_____
_____
_____
_____
_____
_____
_____
_____

**Mindful Minute:**

Speak one kind truth aloud to yourself, even if it's hard to believe.

**Mantra:**

*My voice matters — even when it shakes.*

**Evening Reflection:**

- **How did it feel to express myself today?**

_____
_____
_____
_____
_____
_____
_____
_____

# DAY 258 — Holding Space for Myself

I've held space for others —
listened without rushing,
stood beside their storms,
offered quiet presence.

But I often forget
to extend the same grace to myself.

Now, I pause.
I listen inward.
I let my emotions rise
without judgment or fixing.

This is what holding space looks like:
meeting myself where I am,
without shame,
without pressure.

It's not selfish.
It's sacred.

**Morning Reflection:**

Before I hold space for others, I must first do it for myself.
I matter, too.

**Prompt:**

- **What do you need today — emotionally, physically, spiritually?**

_____
_____
_____
_____
_____
_____
_____

## Mindful Minute:

Sit quietly with your hand on your heart. Say, "You're safe with me."

## Mantra:

*I deserve the space I give to others.*

**Evening Reflection:**

- **What need did I honor today?**

_____
_____
_____
_____
_____
_____
_____
_____

# DAY 259 — Fully Seen, Fully Me

There was a time I only showed the polished parts —
the strength, the smiles,
the version of me
that felt most acceptable.

But hiding became a habit,
and the mask, too familiar.

Now, I long to be fully seen —
not just for what I do,
but for who I am.

The cracks.
The softness.
The parts still healing.

To be fully seen is risky —
but it's also where real connection lives.

And in that seeing,
I am fully me.

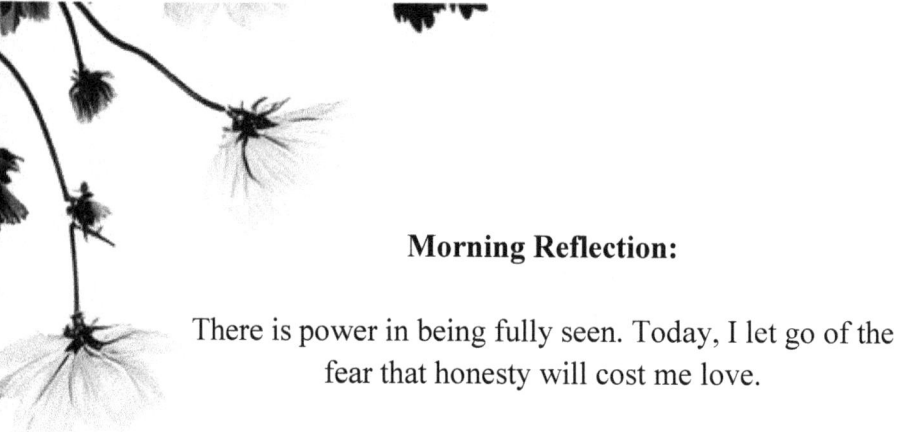

**Morning Reflection:**

There is power in being fully seen. Today, I let go of the fear that honesty will cost me love.

**Prompt:**

- **What would being "fully seen" look like for you?**

_____
_____
_____
_____
_____
_____
_____
_____

**Mindful Minute:**

Imagine standing in a warm light — no hiding, no pretending. Just being.

**Mantra:**

*I am loved as I am, not as I perform.*

**Evening Reflection:**

- How did I show up today without the mask?

_____
_____
_____
_____
_____
_____
_____
_____

# WEEK 38: "The New Standard: Freedom"

This week invites you to define freedom for yourself — not the escape-from-responsibility kind, but the kind rooted in emotional sovereignty. It's about choosing presence over pressure, authenticity over performance, and joy over survival.

# DAY 260 — Redefining Freedom

For so long, I thought freedom meant escape —
from responsibility, from expectations,
from the weight of always being "the strong one."

But I'm learning that true freedom
isn't about running away.

It's about showing up —
authentically, unapologetically,
without shrinking or pretending.

Freedom is choosing rest
without guilt.
Saying no without explanation.
Being loved without performing.

It's not about being untouchable.
It's about being fully human —
and knowing that's more than enough.

### Morning Reflection:

What if freedom isn't about escaping, but about arriving — fully — in your own life?

### Prompt:

- **What version of freedom were you taught, and how has that shaped you?**

_____
_____
_____
_____
_____
_____
_____

### Mindful Minute:

Breathe into your shoulders and imagine tension dissolving. Let yourself feel weightless for one minute.

## Mantra:

*Freedom is being fully me.*

## Evening Reflection:

- **Where did I choose presence over pressure today?**

_____
_____
_____
_____
_____
_____
_____
_____
_____

# DAY 261 — Choosing Me Without Guilt

Choosing yourself isn't selfish.
It's sacred.

There was a time you measured your worth
by how little you needed,
how much you gave,
how invisible you could become
so others could shine.

But self-erasure isn't love.
It's abandonment—of you,
by you.

You're allowed to choose rest over proving,
boundaries over burnout,
truth over pleasing.
You're allowed to want what you want
and still be good.

Today, let "yes" be honest.
Let "no" be holy.
Let choosing yourself
be an act of quiet courage.

**Morning Reflection:**

Saying "yes" to me isn't a betrayal of others. It's an act of courage.

**Prompt:**

- **When was the last time you chose yourself without guilt?**

_____
_____
_____
_____
_____
_____
_____
_____

- **How did it feel?**

_____
_____
_____
_____
_____

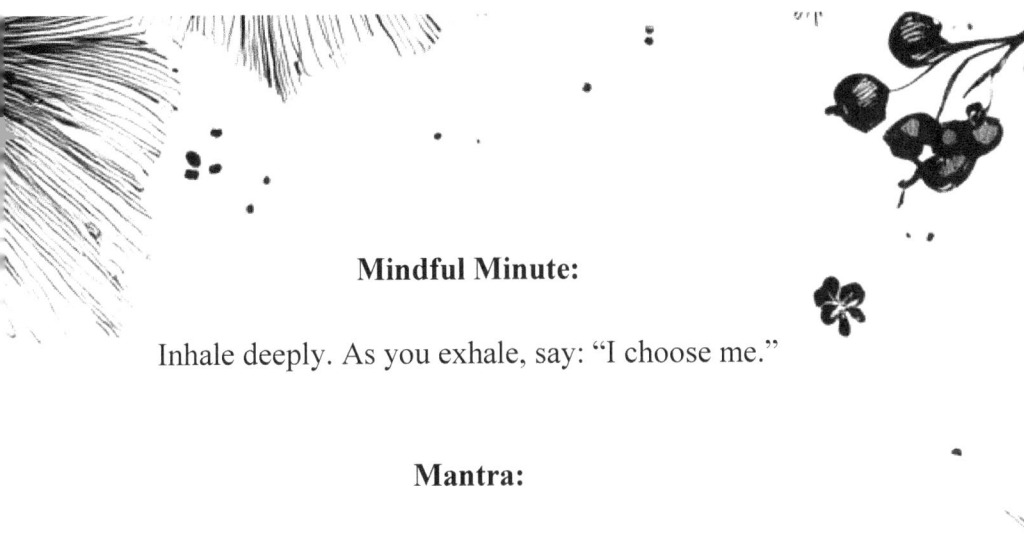

### Mindful Minute:

Inhale deeply. As you exhale, say: "I choose me."

### Mantra:

*My needs are not a burden.*

**Evening Reflection:**

- **What small decision today honored my inner truth?**

_____
_____
_____
_____
_____
_____
_____

# DAY 262 — Free From Old Narratives

There was a time I measured myself by someone else's ruler.
A voice not mine dictated who I could be,
what I could want,
and how much of myself was "too much."

But those were borrowed beliefs,
handed down by fear, by silence, by culture, by survival.
And I don't have to carry them anymore.

Today, I pause and ask:
*Is this truth or is this inheritance?*
Because not everything passed down deserves a place in my becoming.

I am free to outgrow the old stories.
Free to choose a new way.
Free to live as the man I've always been beneath the noise.

**Morning Reflection:**

Today, I release the story that no longer serves me. I am not the outdated version of myself.

**Prompt:**

- What narrative about yourself are you ready to rewrite?

_____
_____
_____
_____
_____
_____
_____

### Mindful Minute:

Close your eyes. Picture yourself setting down a heavy book titled *Who I Was*. Walk away lighter.

### Mantra:

*I am not who I was. I am who I'm becoming.*

**Evening Reflection:**

- **What belief or story did I challenge today?**

_____
_____
_____
_____
_____
_____
_____
_____

## DAY 263 — Permission to Feel Joy

Joy has not always felt safe.
Sometimes it felt like a setup —
a moment too bright, too loud, too fleeting
to fully trust.

I learned to brace for disappointment,
to downplay delight,
to not laugh too hard or dream too big.
Because what if it all disappears?

But I am learning now
that joy is not a betrayal of the pain I've known.
It's proof that I'm still alive.
That healing is working.
That my heart, though bruised, still opens.

I give myself permission to feel joy —
not because everything is perfect,
but because I no longer need perfection
to feel something beautiful.

**Morning Reflection:**

Joy is not a luxury. It's a necessity. Today, I give myself permission to feel good.

**Prompt:**

- **What brings you joy that you've been denying or minimizing?**

_____
_____
_____
_____
_____
_____
_____

### Mindful Minute:

Smile — even slightly — and hold it for 30 seconds. Let the sensation soften your body.

### Mantra:

*Joy is my birthright.*

**Evening Reflection:**

- **Where did I let joy touch my life today?**

_____
_____
_____
_____
_____
_____
_____
_____

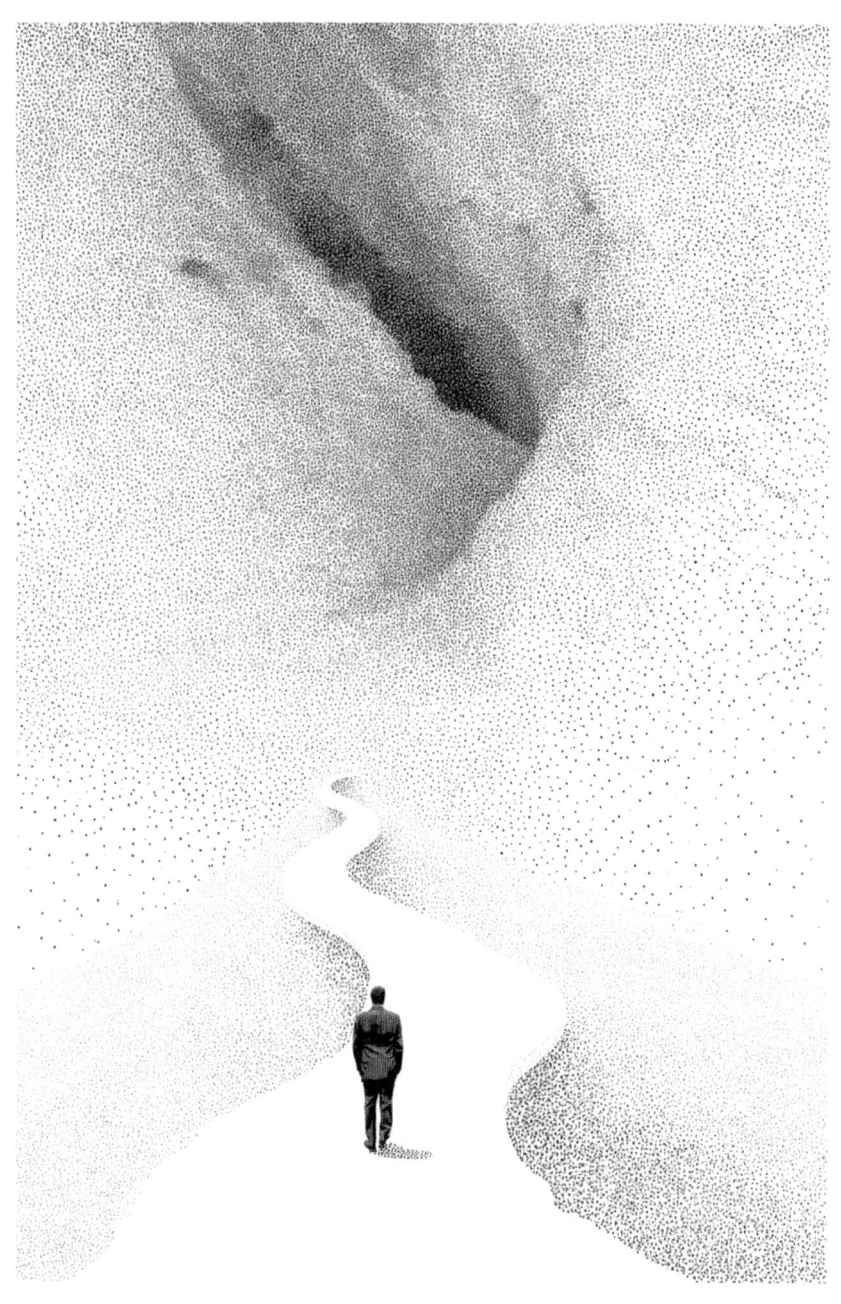

# DAY 264 — Saying No is Saying Yes

Every *no* I speak
used to carry guilt—
as if I was disappointing the world,
as if boundaries were betrayal.

But now I see the truth:
Saying *no* isn't rejection.
It's redirection.
It's making space for what actually matters.
It's honoring my time, my energy, my values.

When I say *no* to what drains me,
I say *yes* to what restores me.
When I say *no* to pressure,
I say *yes* to peace.
When I say *no* to performing,
I say *yes* to authenticity.

Saying *no* is not selfish.
It is sacred.
It is the beginning of a more honest life.
One where I get to show up fully—
because I'm no longer pouring from empty.

**Morning Reflection:**

Every "no" to pressure is a "yes" to freedom. Today, I will say "no" without apology.

**Prompt:**

- **What do you need to say "no" to — for the sake of your peace?**

_____
_____
_____
_____
_____
_____
_____
_____

**Mindful Minute:**

Breathe in peace. Exhale the pressure. Say out loud: "No is a full sentence."

**Mantra:**

*My boundaries protect my freedom.*

**Evening Reflection:**

- **What boundary did I reinforce or discover today?**

_____
_____
_____
_____
_____
_____
_____
_____

# DAY 265 — I Don't Owe My Pain to Anyone

I used to think I had to explain it all—
every scar, every silence, every shadow.
That my pain needed to be justified
to be believed.

But I've learned:
My healing is not a performance.
My wounds are not public property.

I don't owe my pain to anyone.
Not the story.
Not the breakdown.
Not the timeline.

Grief, trauma, and transformation
are deeply personal journeys.
I can choose who gets access—
and who doesn't.

Because boundaries are not walls.
They are doors I get to open
on my terms.

And healing doesn't require proof—
only presence.

## Morning Reflection:

Healing isn't always loud. I don't need to explain the ways I'm growing.

## Prompt:

- **Where do you feel pressured to prove or justify your healing?**

_____
_____
_____
_____
_____
_____
_____
_____

## Mindful Minute:

Rest your hands on your lap. Let yourself be still, even in discomfort.

**Mantra:**

*My healing belongs to me.*

**Evening Reflection:**

- **Did I honor my process without over-explaining?**

_____
_____
_____
_____
_____
_____
_____
_____

# DAY 266 — Free to Begin Again

Some chapters ended before I was ready.
Some doors closed while I was still reaching for the handle.
But that doesn't mean the story is over.

I am not bound by who I used to be,
or what didn't work out.

Growth is not always loud.
Sometimes, it's simply deciding:
*I get to try again.*

There is no shame in starting over.
No weakness in turning the page.
No failure in choosing differently.

Today, I give myself permission—
to release the pressure,
to loosen the grip,
and to begin again.

Freely. Gently. Bravely.

**Morning Reflection:**

Each day is a reset. I am allowed to start again — without shame.

**Prompt:**

- What part of your life are you ready to approach with fresh eyes?

_____
_____
_____
_____
_____
_____
_____

## Mindful Minute:

Breathe in: *"New beginning."*

Breathe out: *"Old story released."*

## Mantra:

*I begin again — fully free.*

**Evening Reflection:**

- What did I forgive myself for today?

_____
_____
_____
_____
_____
_____
_____

# WEEK 39 — Reclaiming Joy

"Joy isn't childish. It's courageous."

Men are often taught that seriousness equals strength — that smiling too much, laughing too loud, or enjoying too deeply is weakness. This week, we're here to reclaim joy as a radical act of healing. You are allowed to be light again.

# DAY 267 — I Am Allowed to Enjoy My Life

Joy doesn't need justification.
It doesn't have to be earned through pain,
or balanced out with struggle.

Somewhere along the way,
I learned to brace for impact
whenever life felt *too good*.
As if happiness was a setup.
As if delight had a cost.

But joy is not a trap.
It's a birthright.
A healing in motion.

I am allowed to enjoy my life—
not just survive it,
not just fix it,
not just explain it.

But to *live it*.
To laugh without apology.
To rest without guilt.
To celebrate without shrinking.

This too, is healing.

**Morning Reflection:**

Your joy isn't irresponsible. It's part of your wholeness.

**Prompt:**

- **What parts of life have you been holding back from fully enjoying?**

_____
_____
_____
_____
_____
_____
_____
_____

### Mindful Minute:

Close your eyes and smile — even slightly. Stay with the sensation for 60 seconds.

### Mantra:

*Joy is not a threat. It's a gift.*

**Evening Reflection:**

- **What moment made me feel alive today?**

_____
_____
_____
_____
_____
_____
_____

# DAY 268 — Joy After Pain

There was a time I couldn't imagine joy.
Not because I didn't want it—
but because pain had taken up all the space.
Grief sat heavy in my chest.
Loss echoed in every quiet moment.

But pain didn't get the final word.

Joy didn't arrive all at once.
It tiptoed back in—
through a familiar song,
the warmth of a friend's laugh,
the quiet beauty of an ordinary day.

Joy after pain isn't naive.
It's sacred.
Hard-won.
A testament to what I've survived.

I don't have to choose between remembering what hurt
and embracing what heals.

I can carry the story—
and still let the light in.

**Morning Reflection:**

Pain may shape you, but joy has the power to rebuild you.

**Prompt:**

- How have you been afraid to feel good again after pain?

_____
_____
_____
_____
_____
_____
_____

**Mindful Minute:**

Place a hand over your heart. Whisper: "I am safe to feel good."

**Mantra:**

*My joy does not betray my past.*

**Evening Reflection:**

- **What happiness did I allow today, even if only for a moment?**

_____
_____
_____
_____
_____
_____
_____

# DAY 269 — Joy in the Ordinary

Not every joy has to be loud.
Some joys arrive without fanfare—
a quiet morning,
a cup of something warm,
a moment of laughter that doesn't ask for more.

For so long, I chased the big highs,
thinking joy had to be earned or extravagant.
But I was missing the kind that doesn't need proving—
the joy found in simply being here.

Joy in the ordinary isn't lesser.
It's steady.
It's grounding.
It's the kind that carries me through.

I don't need fireworks to feel full.
Sometimes, peace is the celebration.

**Morning Reflection:**

Extraordinary happiness often hides in ordinary moments.

**Prompt:**

- **What mundane things bring you unexpected joy?**

_____
_____
_____
_____
_____
_____
_____

## Mindful Minute:

Sip something warm. Do it slowly. Let it feel sacred.

**Mantra:**

*There is beauty in my everyday.*

**Evening Reflection:**

- **What small thing brought unexpected comfort today?**

# DAY 270 — Play Without Performance

Somewhere along the way, play became a performance.
A way to impress.
To compete.
To prove I had value through outcomes and applause.

But play was never meant to be a test.
It was once freedom.
Laughter without agenda.
Movement without measurement.

I miss the version of me who could be silly without shame.
Curious without a goal.
Present without performing.

Today, I give myself permission to return to that version.
To play just because.
To create without critique.
To enjoy without earning.

Joy doesn't need an audience.
Play doesn't need a purpose.
And I don't need to perform to be worthy of delight.

### Morning Reflection:

You don't have to earn playfulness. It's your right.

**Prompt:**

- **What did you used to do just for fun — without needing to be "good" at it?**

_____
_____
_____
_____
_____
_____
_____
_____

### Mindful Minute:

Stretch your arms like a kid waking up. Let yourself feel silly. Smile freely.

### Mantra:

*I give myself permission to play.*

**Evening Reflection:**

- **When did I feel most light-hearted today?**

_____
_____
_____
_____
_____
_____
_____
_____

# DAY 271 — Laughter is Liberation

There are moments when laughter breaks through like light—
sudden, unfiltered, and true.
And for a moment, the weight lifts.
The armor slips.
The world softens.

Laughter is more than noise.
It's release.
It's resistance.
It's remembering I'm still human underneath the pressure.

In laughter, I find pieces of myself untouched by shame.
Not trying to prove.
Not trying to perform.
Just being.

Today, I welcome the kind of joy that doesn't ask permission.
The kind that bubbles up from somewhere deeper than logic.
Laughter that says,
"I'm alive. I'm healing. I'm free."

Even if the world feels heavy—
my laughter can still be a rebellion.

### Morning Reflection:

Laughter releases what words can't.

**Prompt:**

- **When was the last time you laughed so hard you forgot the weight of your life?**

_____
_____
_____
_____
_____
_____
_____
_____

### Mindful Minute:

Recall a funny memory. Let your face react. Let your chest soften.

### Mantra:

*My joy is revolutionary.*

**Evening Reflection:**

- **Who or what brought me joy today?**

_____
_____
_____
_____
_____
_____
_____

# DAY 272 — You Deserve to Celebrate

Not because you crossed the finish line.
Not because everything is perfect.
But because you've made it this far.

You've endured quiet battles no one saw.
You've healed in places still tender.
You've shown up, even when it felt easier to hide.

Celebration isn't reserved for milestones.
It's a way of honoring your becoming.
Of saying, "This version of me matters too."

You don't have to wait for permission.
You don't need the world's applause.
Today, your breath is enough reason.
Your softness is worth toasting.

You deserve to celebrate — not later, but now.

**Morning Reflection:**

You don't need permission to celebrate your progress.

**Prompt:**

- What personal win (big or small) deserves to be honored right now?

_____
_____
_____
_____
_____
_____
_____
_____

### Mindful Minute:

Clasp your hands. Whisper, "I see you," like you're talking to your past self.

### Mantra:

*I honor my journey with joy.*

**Evening Reflection:**

- What part of myself did I celebrate today?

_____
_____
_____
_____
_____
_____
_____
_____

# DAY 273 — Joy Is Also Masculine

Somewhere along the way, we were taught
that joy didn't belong to men —
that laughter had to be muted,
that delight made us less grounded,
that too much lightness made us look soft.

But joy is not weakness.
It is not frivolous.
It is not a betrayal of strength.

Joy is resistance.
It is healing.
It is wholeness in motion.

To smile without apology.
To dance without rhythm.
To feel warmth rise in your chest
and not push it down —
this is masculine too.

There is courage in choosing joy.
Power in softness.
Masculinity that doesn't need armor.

Joy fits you — just as you are.

## Morning Reflection:

Joy isn't soft. It's strong. Especially when chosen on purpose.

## Prompt:

- **What are some joyful traits you admire in men — and in yourself?**

_____
_____
_____
_____
_____
_____
_____
_____

## Mindful Minute:

Inhale deeply. On the exhale, let go of the belief that joy makes you weak.

## Mantra:

*My strength includes my joy.*

**Evening Reflection:**

- **Where did I express joyful masculinity today?**

_____
_____
_____
_____
_____
_____
_____
_____

# Month 9 Reflection: Restoration

1. **What Rest Has Looked Like This Month**

- Did you rest? If not, why? If yes, how did it help?

_____
_____
_____
_____
_____
_____
_____
_____

# WEEK 40 — Building an Emotional Legacy

"What you pass down doesn't have to be pain."

This week is about shifting what we leave behind — not just in property or provision, but in presence. Emotional legacy is the imprint of how you made others feel, how safe you were for yourself and those around you, and how deeply you allowed love to live in your life. You are building something worth remembering.

# DAY 274 — Legacy Isn't Just Material

We often measure legacy in wealth,
in buildings named after us,
in land, in titles, in what we can leave behind.

But legacy is also
how your child feels when they see you.
It's the tone you use when you speak.
It's the safety someone remembers
when they were with you.

Legacy is emotional inheritance.
Did they feel seen in your
presence?
Did you model gentleness with yourself?
Did you love in a way that made others softer?

What you leave behind
is not always what can be counted —
but what can be felt for generations.

Let your legacy be a feeling.
Let it be healing.
Let it be whole

**Morning Reflection:**

You won't be remembered for the things you owned, but for how you showed up.

**Prompt:**

- **What kind of emotional legacy do you want to leave behind?**

_____
_____
_____
_____
_____
_____
_____
_____

### Mindful Minute:

Visualize someone you care about feeling safe in your presence. Let that picture settle in your chest.

### Mantra:

*I am building a legacy of peace.*

**Evening Reflection:**

- What part of my emotional legacy did I nurture today?

_____
_____
_____
_____
_____
_____
_____
_____

# DAY 275: The Power of Emotional Inheritance

Not all inheritance is visible.
Some of the most lasting things
are passed down in silence.

The way you flinch at kindness.
The way you hold your breath in chaos.
The way you apologize for existing.

These didn't start with you —
they were taught, modeled,
handed down like heirlooms.

But so can peace.
So can softness.
So can joy without fear.

You have the power to pass down
more than survival.
You can give rest.
You can give warmth.

**Morning Reflection:**

Your emotional health teaches others how to carry theirs.

**Prompt:**

- What emotional patterns did you inherit?

_____
_____
_____
_____
_____
_____
_____

- Which ones are you breaking?

_____
_____
_____
_____
_____
_____
_____

**Mindful Minute:**

Breathe deeply and say: "I am allowed to do things differently."

**Mantra:**

*I choose what continues through me.*

**Evening Reflection:**

- **What generational chain did I loosen today?**

_____
_____
_____
_____
_____
_____
_____

# DAY 276 — Living as an Example

Someone is always watching —
not with judgment, but with hope.

The way you pause to breathe,
the way you speak kindly to yourself,
the way you ask for help
instead of pretending you're fine —
these are lessons someone else is learning.

You don't need a platform
to lead by example.
You just need presence,
honesty,
and the courage
to live what you believe.

Your healing teaches.
Your softness teaches.
Your joy teaches.

Even when you don't see it —
you're showing the way.

**Morning Reflection:**

You don't have to preach healing — just live it.

**Prompt:**

- **What would it look like to model emotional openness today?**

_____
_____
_____
_____
_____
_____

**Mindful Minute:**

Sit upright. Let your shoulders relax. Practice being available.

**Mantra:**

*My healing teaches in silence.*

**Evening Reflection:**

- **How did I lead with emotional courage today?**

_____
_____
_____
_____
_____
_____
_____
_____

# DAY 277 — How You Make Others Feel

People may forget your words.
They may forget what you did.
But they rarely forget how you made them feel.

Did you offer safety or pressure?
Did your presence invite honesty,
or did it demand performance?

Masculinity isn't measured
by how loud you speak,
but by how deeply others can exhale around you.

Kindness leaves a mark.
So does judgment.

You don't have to be perfect.
Just aware.
Just present.
Just willing to let your softness speak.

**Morning Reflection:**

People may forget your words, but they'll remember your energy.

**Prompt:**

- **How do people feel when they leave your presence? How would you like them to feel?**

_____
_____
_____
_____
_____
_____
_____
_____

### Mindful Minute:

Place your hand over your chest and say, "I am a safe place."

**Mantra:**

*My presence is powerful.*

**Evening Reflection:**

- **Who felt safe with me today — and why?**

_____
_____
_____
_____
_____
_____
_____
_____

# DAY 278 — The Love You Leave Behind

In the end, it won't be the titles or trophies.
It'll be the quiet moments.
The steady hands.
The words you didn't rush.
The hugs you meant.

Legacy isn't just what you build —
it's what you nurture.
It's the love you leave behind
in the hearts of those who felt safe with you.

You don't have to be known by many.
Just deeply known by a few.
And in that, you've done something eternal.

**Morning Reflection:**

The greatest legacy is love that outlives you.

**Prompt:**

- **What acts of love have left the biggest imprint on your life?**

_____
_____
_____
_____
_____
_____
_____
_____

**Mindful Minute:**

Recall someone who made you feel deeply loved. Let yourself smile.

**Mantra:**

*I give the love I wish I received.*

**Evening Reflection:**

- What loving act did I offer without expectation today?

_____
_____
_____
_____
_____
_____
_____

# DAY 279 — Legacy in Small Moments

Legacy isn't always loud.
Sometimes, it's the quiet check-in.
The listening ear.
The smile that says, *"I see you."*

It's not measured in monuments
but in memories.
In the way someone feels safe
because you made space.

The small moments —
they echo longer than we know.
And sometimes, they're the most lasting things we leave behind.

**Morning Reflection:**

Legacy lives in the tiny, consistent things — not just grand gestures.

**Prompt:**

- **What quiet or unnoticed things do you do that express care and character?**

_____
_____
_____
_____
_____
_____
_____
_____

**Mindful Minute:**

As you sit quietly, list 3 quiet ways you've shown love this week.

**Mantra:**

*My smallest efforts still matter.*

**Evening Reflection:**

- **What small gesture today said, "I care"?**

_____
_____
_____
_____
_____
_____
_____
_____

# DAY 280 — Becoming the Man You Needed

You may not have had him.
The one who saw you.
Who held your fear with tenderness,
and your dreams without judgment.

But you can become him.

With every healed wound,
every boundary honored,
every tear allowed,
you are building him —
from your own bravery.

Becoming the man
your younger self waited for
is the most sacred kind of redemption.

**Morning Reflection:**

You are free to become what you once lacked.

**Prompt:**

- **What would your younger self be proud of today?**

_____
_____
_____
_____
_____
_____
_____

## Mindful Minute:

Picture your younger self smiling at you. Breathe into that connection.

## Mantra:

*I am becoming the man I needed.*

## Evening Reflection:

- **How did I honor my younger self today?**

_____
_____
_____
_____
_____
_____
_____
_____

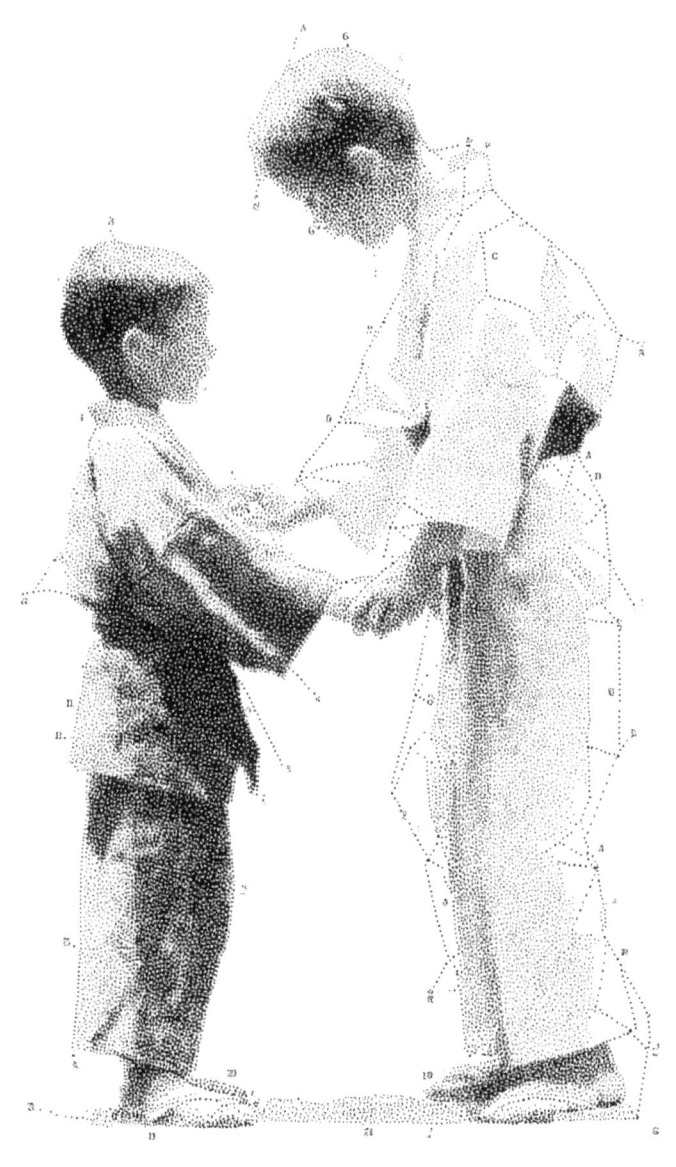

# WEEK 41 — The Currency of Your Presence

*"Presence is the rarest and most powerful form of generosity."*

This week focuses on your presence — the quality of attention and energy you bring to each moment. Your presence can soothe, inspire, heal, or harm. It is your greatest offering. Let's explore how to be more grounded, intentional, and available.

## DAY 281 — Presence Is Generosity

You don't have to give answers.
You don't have to perform wisdom.
You don't have to fix what hurts.

Your presence —
undistracted, unrushed, undivided —
is already a gift.

In a world that hurries and hurries,
your stillness speaks.
In a culture that talks over pain,
your listening heals.

Being fully here is not small.
It's generosity.
It's love without noise.

### Morning Reflection:

Sometimes, the most generous thing you can offer is your full attention.

**Prompt:**

- **When was the last time someone truly listened to you? How did it feel?**

_____
_____
_____
_____
_____
_____
_____

**Mindful Minute:**

Spend one full minute observing your surroundings — no judgment, just presence.

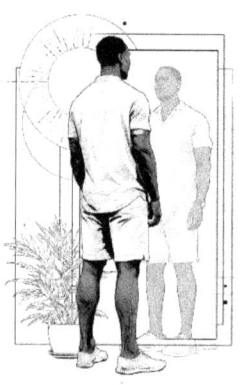

**Mantra:**

*My presence is a gift.*

**Evening Reflection:**

- **Where did I show up fully today?**

_____
_____
_____
_____
_____
_____
_____
_____

# DAY 282 — Distracted or Devoted?

### Morning Reflection:

Distraction is the enemy of presence — it steals our now.

### Prompt:

- **What habits keep you from being fully present with the people you love?**

_____
_____
_____
_____
_____
_____
_____
_____

### Mindful Minute:

Turn off all devices. Close your eyes.

Breathe and repeat: "I am here."

**Mantra:**

*I choose connection over distraction.*

**Evening Reflection:**

- **When did I resist distraction today — and what changed?**

_____
_____
_____
_____
_____
_____
_____
_____

# DAY 283 — Presence with Self

It's easy to show up for others.
To be the safe place.
The listener.
The one who holds it all.

But what about you?

Presence with self
means turning that same kindness inward.
Noticing when you're tired,
when you're overwhelmed,
when you're silently asking for rest.

It means sitting with your feelings
without needing to fix them.
It's hearing your own voice
before the world's.

Being present with yourself
isn't selfish.
It's sacred.
It's where true wholeness begins.

## Morning Reflection:

You cannot be present for others if you abandon yourself.

**Prompt:**

- **What parts of yourself do you tend to ignore or avoid?**

_____
_____
_____
_____
_____
_____
_____
_____

## Mindful Minute:

**Ask:** "How am I really doing?"

Stay present with the honest answer.

## Mantra:

*I return to myself with care.*

**Evening Reflection:**

- **Did I check in with myself today — even briefly?**

_____
_____
_____
_____
_____
_____
_____

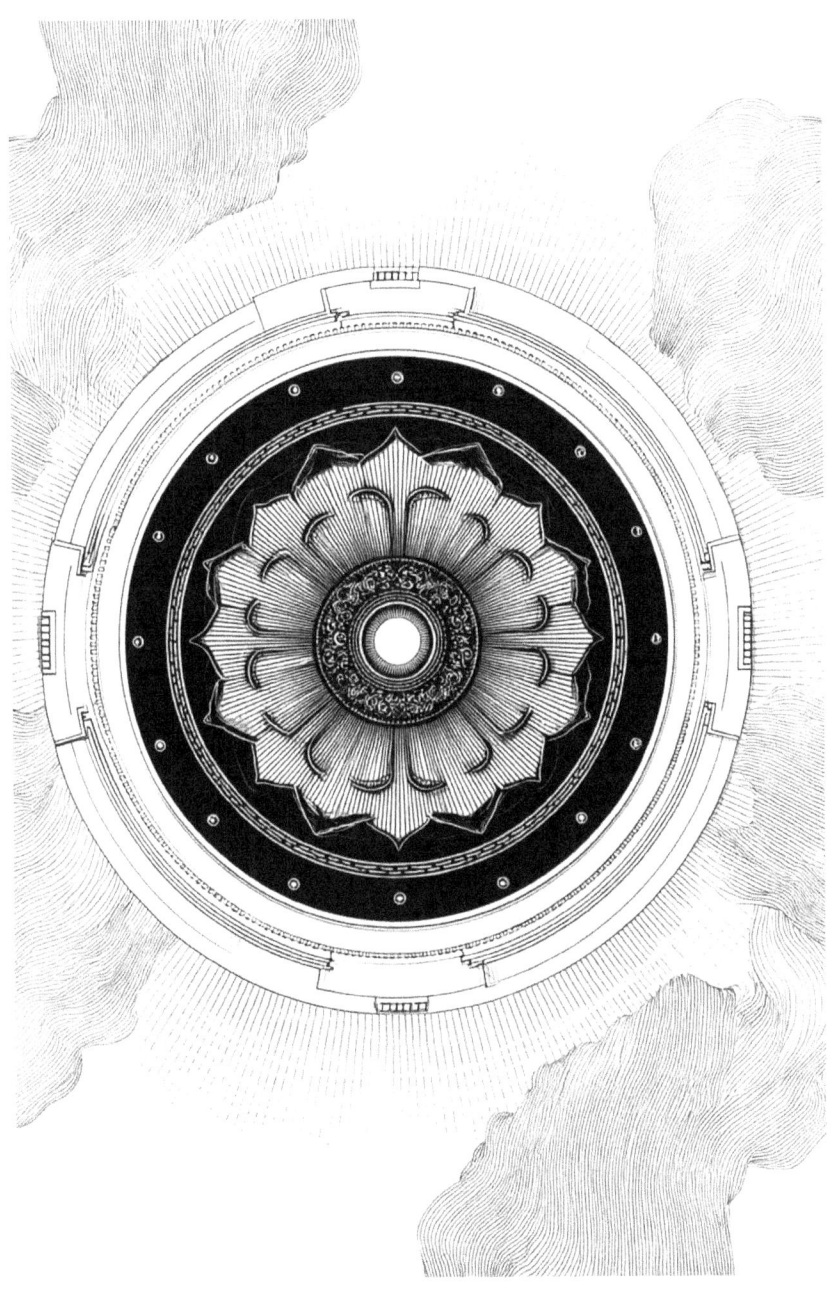

# DAY 284 — Eye Contact and Heart Contact

Sometimes the most powerful moments
don't need words.

A glance held a second longer.
A look that says, *I see you.*
Not for what you do —
but for who you are beneath it all.

Eye contact can feel exposing,
especially when you're used to hiding.
It invites truth.
It invites presence.
It invites the possibility of being known.

But real connection goes deeper —
beyond just seeing,
to **feeling with**.
That's heart contact.

To meet another person's eyes
and let your walls fall
isn't weakness.
It's the beginning of belonging.
To  them.
To yourself.

### Morning Reflection:

Real connection starts with slowing down enough to see and be seen.

**Prompt:**

- **Who in your life deserves more undivided attention?**

_____
_____
_____
_____
_____
_____
_____

### Mindful Minute:

Practice softening your gaze and relaxing your face. Let your energy say, "I see you."

### Mantra:

*I make space for connection.*

**Evening Reflection:**

- **Where did I offer intentional attention today?**

_____
_____
_____
_____
_____
_____
_____

# DAY 285 — Being Where Your Feet Are

Peace often isn't found in the next big thing.
It's found right here —
in the now.
In the quiet moment before the phone rings.
In the breath before a reply.
In the space between one step and the next.

"Being where your feet are" means returning
to the only place life actually happens —
the present.

Not racing ahead to fix tomorrow.
Not replaying what went wrong yesterday.
But *being here*
— fully —
in your body, in this moment.

It's in the feel of the ground holding you up.
The breath that reminds you:
you're alive.
You're safe.
You're becoming.

Presence isn't passive.
It's the most powerful place to live from.
So when the world pulls you in every direction, remember:
you only ever need to be
where your feet are.

## Morning Reflection:

You cannot live your life if you're always trying to escape it.

**Prompt:**

- **Where are you emotionally living today — the past, the future, or the present?**

_____
_____
_____
_____
_____
_____
_____

### Mindful Minute:

Press your feet into the ground.

Feel supported. Say aloud, "I am here."

### Mantra:

*I live in the moment, not in my mind.*

### Evening Reflection:

- **Did I truly inhabit my life today?**

_____
_____
_____
_____
_____
_____
_____

# DAY 286 — Holding Space

Holding space isn't about having the perfect words.
It's not about fixing, solving, or performing wisdom.
It's about presence.
About staying — especially when it's hard.

To hold space is to offer your quiet,
your attention,
your non-judgment,
your breath —
when someone else is unraveling.

It says:
"I'm not here to rescue you,
but I *am* here to walk with you."

Sometimes, holding space means
letting silence stretch without rushing to fill it.
Other times, it's asking,
"What do you need?"
and being okay when the answer is
"I don't know."

You can hold space for others.
And you can hold it for yourself.
To feel.
To process.
To be seen — even if only by your own eyes.

To hold space is an act of love.
Not loud.

Not showy.
But sacred.

**Morning Reflection:**

Presence isn't always about fixing — sometimes it's just about witnessing.

**Prompt:**

- Who in your life needs less advice and more quiet presence from you?

_____
_____
_____
_____
_____
_____
_____

**Mindful Minute:**

Practice being with silence. Let go of the urge to respond.

**Mantra:**

*I hold space with strength and softness.*

**Evening Reflection:**

- **How did I make someone feel safe today?**

_____
_____
_____
_____
_____
_____
_____
_____

# DAY 287 — The Quality of Presence

Presence isn't just about being in the room —
it's about how you *show up* in it.

You can be physically present
but emotionally unavailable.
You can sit beside someone
and still feel miles apart.

The quality of presence is measured
not by time, but by intention.
By how softly you listen.
By whether your eyes hold theirs
without scanning for escape.
By how safe someone feels
being fully themselves near you.

Presence says:
"I am here, with you, not just around you."
It's attention without agenda.
Stillness without discomfort.
Compassion without condition.

And the same applies to yourself.
Are you present with your own heart?
Or do you rush past your emotions,
always chasing the next thing?

Presence is the gift that makes people exhale.
It's not something you perform —
it's something you *offer*.

Quiet.
Anchored.
Real.

**Morning Reflection:**

It's not how much time you give, but how deeply you show up.

**Prompt:**

- **What does "high-quality" presence mean to you? How can you bring more of it?**

_____
_____
_____
_____
_____
_____
_____

**Mindful Minute:**

Focus on your breath, then gently bring your awareness to your heartbeat.

**Mantra:**

*I bring all of me to the moment.*

**Evening Reflection:**

- **Where did I give quality over quantity today?**

_____
_____
_____
_____
_____
_____
_____

# WEEK 42 — The Version of Me I'm Becoming

*"Healing isn't about becoming someone else. It's about returning to who you really are."*

This week invites you to gently step into the future version of yourself — not one molded by pressure or performance, but one shaped by intention, clarity, and wholeness. It's time to meet the man you're becoming.

## DAY 288 — Becoming on Purpose

You are always becoming —
but are you becoming *on purpose*?

So much of life shapes us without permission.
Experiences, expectations, survival.
We adapt. We cope.
We become what the world demands —
but not always who we *desire* to be.

Becoming on purpose means choosing.
Not just reacting, but responding.
Not just adjusting, but *aligning*.

**It means asking:**

- Who am I underneath all this noise?
- What values do I want to embody?
- What kind of man am I building, moment by moment?

Becoming on purpose is slow.
Intentional. Disruptive, even.
Because it requires unlearning roles
you never asked to audition for.

It's not about performance.
It's about *presence*.
Choosing character over comfort.
Choosing healing over hiding.
Choosing meaning over momentum.

You don't have to have it all figured out.
But you *do* get to decide:
"This is who I'm becoming —
and I'm choosing it every day."

**Morning Reflection:**

We are always becoming something — the question is, are we choosing it?

**Prompt:**

- If you lived more intentionally, what would your days look and feel like?

_____
_____
_____
_____
_____
_____
_____
_____

**Mindful Minute:**

Close your eyes and breathe deeply. Picture yourself six months from now — grounded, healed, and aligned.

**Mantra:**

*I am becoming on purpose.*

**Evening Reflection:**

- **What choices today reflected the man I want to become?**

_____
_____
_____
_____
_____
_____
_____
_____

# DAY 289 — Meeting Future Me

Who am I becoming?

Not in theory.
Not in fantasy.
But in quiet, ordinary choices made today.

The future version of me isn't waiting
in some distant, polished perfection.
He is being built — here, now —
in the ways I show up,
the boundaries I honor,
the truths I speak,
and the lies I stop telling myself.

Meeting future me
isn't a one-time event —
it's a practice of presence.

It's imagining him not as someone
*better,*
but someone *braver.*
Not richer, or louder, or more impressive —
but freer.
More whole.
At peace with his past
and aligned with his values.

So I ask:
What would future me thank me for today?

Maybe it's rest.
Maybe it's courage.
Maybe it's finally letting go of what no longer fits.

He's not far away.
He's being formed in this moment —
through each conscious choice to grow,
heal,
and live with intention.

**Morning Reflection:**

The man you're becoming isn't out of reach — he's waiting for you to align with him.

**Prompt:**

- Write a letter from your future self to your current self. What does he know that you don't?

_____
_____
_____
_____
_____
_____
_____
_____

**Mindful Minute:**

Sit in stillness. Whisper to yourself: "Show me who I am becoming."

**Mantra:**

*My future is shaped by my presence today.*

**Evening Reflection:**

- What did I learn about myself today?

_____
_____
_____
_____
_____
_____
_____
_____

# DAY 290 — Old Scripts, New Chapters

I've lived by stories I didn't write.
Inherited lines whispered in silence,
engraved in glances,
handed down through expectation.

Scripts that told me who I should be —
strong but silent,
capable but never in need,
present but never too visible.

But I am learning:
I can hold the wisdom of the past
without reenacting its pain.
I can honor where I came from
without staying stuck in who I had to be.

The old script said: *Don't feel too much.*
This new chapter says: *Your emotions are sacred.*

The old script said: *Prove your worth.*
This new chapter says: *You already have it.*

The old script said: *Shrink to fit in.*
This new chapter says: *Expand to be free.*

Today, I turn the page.
Not with anger — but with intention.
I choose to write my next chapter in truth,

with softness, with honesty,
with the kind of courage that liberates,
not just me — but those who'll read this life I'm writing.

### Morning Reflection:

You can't write a new story if you keep reading from the same script.

**Prompt:**

- **What outdated beliefs or behaviors are still narrating your life?**

_____
_____
_____
_____
_____
_____
_____

### Mindful Minute:

Breathe into your heart space. Imagine yourself releasing one old script that no longer serves you.

### Mantra:

*I rewrite my story with truth and tenderness.*

### Evening Reflection:

- **What limiting belief did I challenge today?**

_____
_____
_____
_____
_____
_____
_____

# DAY 291: Becoming Doesn't Require Burning

I used to think that growth meant destruction.
That I had to torch my past
to make room for my future.
That in order to become someone new,
I had to reject who I had been.

But I'm learning that evolution
can be rooted in compassion,
not combustion.

I don't have to burn it all down
to move forward.
I can carry parts of me with grace—
the missteps, the questions,
the younger versions of myself
who only knew how to survive.

Becoming doesn't always mean breaking.
Sometimes it looks like gentle unfolding.
Like softening into truth.
Like releasing shame, not identity.
Like integrating, not erasing.

Today, I remind myself:
I can bloom without scorched earth.
I can heal without hating who I was.
I can rise without rubble.

## Morning Reflection:

Transformation doesn't always require destruction.
Sometimes it just takes permission.

**Prompt:**

- **Where have you made progress without pain — and overlooked it because it was gentle?**

_____
_____
_____
_____
_____
_____
_____
_____

## Mindful Minute:

Breathe gently. With each exhale, say silently, "I give myself permission to evolve with ease."

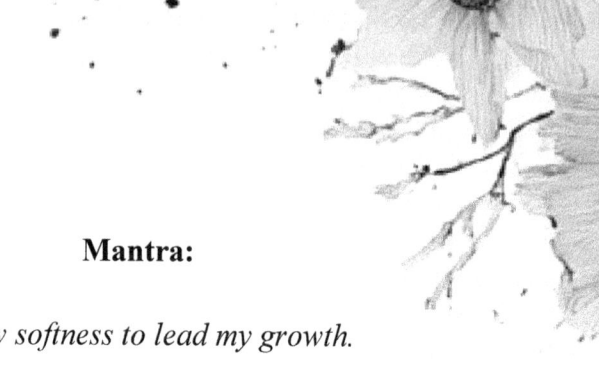

### Mantra:

*I allow softness to lead my growth.*

### Evening Reflection:

- **Where did I practice gentle evolution today?**

_____
_____
_____
_____
_____
_____
_____
_____

# DAY 292 — A New Definition of Strength

Strength isn't always loud.
It doesn't always show up with clenched fists and a voice that dominates the room.
Sometimes, strength is the whisper that says, "I don't have to prove anything today."

It's in the man who chooses patience over power.
The one who apologizes first.
Who admits when he's wrong.
Who cries without shame, and listens without needing to fix.

This strength doesn't wear armor;
it wears softness as a shield.
It walks away from battles that only feed ego
and leans into connection, even when it's uncomfortable.

This is the strength I'm learning to embody:
not performative, but rooted.
Not reactionary, but aware.
Not rigid, but resilient.

A strength that doesn't just protect —
but heals.
And frees.
And welcomes.

**Morning Reflection:**

- What if your strength is in your softness, your steadiness, your self-awareness?

_____
_____
_____
_____
_____
_____
_____

**Prompt:**

- What does strength look like in the version of you you're becoming?

_____
_____
_____
_____
_____
_____
_____

**Mindful Minute:**

Sit upright. Inhale strength. Exhale softness. Repeat slowly.

**Mantra:**

*My strength is rooted in truth, not tension.*

**Evening Reflection:**

- **Where did I feel strong today — without force?**

_____
_____
_____
_____
_____
_____
_____
_____

# DAY 293 — The Inner Compass

There comes a time when external voices grow too loud —
everyone has an opinion, a direction, a "should."
But deep within me, there's a quieter voice.
One that doesn't shout but *knows*.

This is my inner compass.
It isn't fueled by fear or pressure.
It doesn't operate from guilt, comparison, or urgency.
It speaks in alignment, not approval.

It's the part of me that remembers who I am beneath all the roles I play.
The place where intuition lives —
where peace lives —
where truth is not something to chase, but something to return to.

When I pause long enough to listen,
I find I've always had what I needed to decide:
not the easiest path,
but the *truest* one.

From this place, I move forward —
not perfectly, but *authentically*.
Guided, not by what's loudest,
but by what's *deepest*.

## Morning Reflection:

You don't need more advice — you need more alignment.

## Prompt:

- **What decisions are waiting for you to come home to yourself first?**

_____
_____
_____
_____
_____
_____
_____

## Mindful Minute:

Place your hand over your heart.

Ask, "What do I need to hear right now?" Listen.

### Mantra:

*I trust the quiet wisdom within.*

### Evening Reflection:

- **What internal cue did I honor today?**

_____
_____
_____
_____
_____
_____
_____
_____

# DAY 294 — Becoming Whole, Not Perfect

There was a time I chased perfection—
believing that flawlessness was the goal,
that being worthy meant being without cracks,
that love had to be earned through performance.

But I was never meant to be a masterpiece behind glass.
I was meant to be *alive*—
complex, honest, unfinished.
I was meant to grow, to heal, to unravel and rebuild.

Perfection keeps me hiding.
Wholeness invites me home.

Wholeness says:
You can bring all of you here—
the messy, the magical, the misunderstood.
You don't need to be edited to be embraced.

I am not a project.
I am a person.
And every piece of me—
even the ones I once tried to erase—
belong in the story of becoming whole.

**Morning Reflection:**

You're not here to become flawless. You're here to become whole.

**Prompt:**

- **Where have you confused perfection with growth?**

_____
_____
_____
_____
_____
_____
_____

**Mindful Minute:**

Breathe in wholeness. Exhale judgment. Place a hand on your chest and simply repeat: "I am enough."

**Mantra:**

*I choose wholeness over perfection.*

**Evening Reflection:**

- **What did I accept about myself today?**

_____
_____
_____
_____
_____
_____
_____
_____

# WEEK 43 — The Unwritten Letter

"Sometimes, the healing begins with the words you never said."

This week, we open the door to what's been left unsaid — to the letters never written, the truths we swallowed, and the people (including ourselves) we've struggled to be honest with. It's time to give voice to your silence.

## DAY 295 — If I Could Speak Freely

If I could speak freely,
I'd tell you that some days, I'm tired of holding it all together.
That strength isn't always silence—
and silence isn't always peace.

I'd admit the weight I carry behind my smile.
I'd stop performing wellness
and let you see the weather inside me.

If I could speak freely,
I'd say:
I need help sometimes.
I miss softness.
I want to be held, not just respected.

I'd name the dreams I've buried
beneath responsibility and quiet sacrifice.
I'd say no—without apology.
I'd say yes—to the things that scare me with how much I want them.

If I could speak freely,
I'd speak from the scar, not the script.
I'd stop shrinking my truth
to keep others comfortable.

But maybe I can start now—
with a whisper, a breath, a single brave sentence.
Maybe this is where freedom begins.

**Morning Reflection:**

We often silence our most powerful truths to protect others — or ourselves. But unspoken truth still weighs on the soul.

Prompt:

- Who have you withheld honesty from?

_____
_____
_____
_____
_____
_____
_____

- What would you say if you felt safe?

_____
_____
_____
_____
_____
_____
_____

**Mindful Minute:**

Breathe deeply. On the exhale, whisper, "I release what I can no longer carry."

**Mantra:**

*My truth deserves a voice.*

**Evening Reflection:**

- **What did I need to express today, and why didn't I?**

_____
_____
_____
_____
_____
_____
_____
_____

# DAY 296 — The Letter I Never Sent

There's a letter I never sent—
not because I didn't write it,
but because I didn't think I was allowed to speak that
honestly.

It started with "I miss you"
and ended with "I'm sorry."
In between, it carried years of silence,
words I rehearsed in the dark,
and feelings too complicated to package neatly.

I wanted to tell you I was angry.
I wanted to tell you I was hurt.
I wanted you to know how I protected your name
even when mine was being misunderstood.
How I held space for you long after you left mine.

The letter was truth,
raw and unfinished,
with no expectation of reply—
just a longing to be known,
finally, without armor.

But I never sent it.
Maybe because I didn't want to reopen the wound,
or maybe because healing didn't require your presence—
only my permission.

Still, I keep the letter.
Not for you,
but for me—
as proof that I felt,
that I tried,
that I loved enough to write it.

And maybe,
that was the closure I needed all along.

**Morning Reflection:**

There's healing in the unwritten. Closure doesn't always come from conversation — sometimes, it comes from release.

**Prompt:**

**Write a letter you never intend to send. Say everything.**

_____
_____
_____
_____
_____
_____
_____
_____
_____
_____
_____
_____
_____
_____
_____
_____

**Mindful Minute:**

With eyes closed, imagine placing that letter in the hands of the person it's for. Then let go.

**Mantra:**

*I heal even when no one hears me.*

**Evening Reflection:**

- **How did that letter change how I feel?**

_____
_____
_____
_____
_____
_____
_____
_____

# DAY 297 — An Apology to Myself

I'm sorry.
For all the times I quieted my voice
so others could feel more comfortable.
For the moments I carried blame
that never belonged to me.
For shrinking to fit spaces
that never saw my fullness.

I'm sorry for the harsh words I whispered
to the mirror in silence.
For every "not enough" I believed,
for every dream I delayed,
for every part of me I abandoned
in pursuit of being "liked," "good," or "safe."

I'm sorry for calling my needs "too much,"
my rest "laziness,"
my tears "weakness."
I mistook survival for peace.
And I know now,
you were doing the best you could
with what you had.

So here's what I promise:
I will listen more.
I will rest without guilt.
I will celebrate without conditions.

I will treat you—myself—with gentleness,
like someone I truly love.

This isn't the end.
It's the beginning
of a better relationship with myself—
rooted in compassion,
anchored in truth,
and softened by grace.

**Morning Reflection:**

We often demand apologies from others — but sometimes,
we owe them to ourselves first.

**Prompt:**

- **Write an apology to yourself for the times you abandoned, belittled, or betrayed your own needs.**

_____
_____
_____
_____
_____
_____
_____
_____

### Mindful Minute:

Place your hand on your chest. Say: "I'm sorry. I forgive you. I'm listening now."

### Mantra:

*I deserve my own compassion.*

**Evening Reflection:**

- **Did I treat myself more kindly today?**

_____
_____
_____
_____
_____
_____
_____

# DAY 298 — What I Wish I'd Heard

I wish someone had told me:
"You don't have to be everything for everyone."
That being tired doesn't mean I'm failing.
That needing help doesn't make me weak.
That I am allowed to rest
without earning it first.

I wish someone had looked me in the eyes and said:
"You are already enough."
Not because of what you produce,
or how well you perform,
but simply because you exist.
You are worthy.

I wish I'd heard:
"It's okay to cry."
"It's okay to feel lost."
"It's okay to not have all the answers."
I wish someone had said,
"You are not alone in this."

And maybe the person I needed
was the one I'm still becoming.
So today, I say to myself:
"You are seen."

"You are loved."
"You are allowed to be exactly as you are."

These are the words I now speak into the spaces
where silence once echoed.
Words I never heard then—
but choose to believe now.

## Morning Reflection:

Sometimes the healing isn't about what was said, but what was never spoken.

**Prompt:**

- **What words did you long to hear growing up?**

_____
_____
_____
_____
_____
_____
_____

- **From a parent, a partner, or yourself?**

_____
_____
_____
_____
_____
_____
_____

## Mindful Minute:

Say those words to yourself now — even if they feel foreign. Let them land.

## Mantra:

*I can give myself what I once needed from others.*

## Evening Reflection:

- **How did those words affect me today?**

_____
_____
_____
_____
_____
_____
_____

# DAY 299: Dear Younger Me

Dear Younger Me,
I see you—shoulders heavy with invisible weights,
trying so hard to be what everyone needs,
fearing that being *you* might never be enough.
You didn't deserve the silence you sat in,
nor the pressure to grow up too soon.

If I could sit beside you now,
I wouldn't rush you to heal or fix anything.
I'd simply place a hand on your back
and let you know:
You are not broken.
You are learning.
And that is more than enough.

You don't have to be the strong one all the time.
You don't have to make yourself smaller
to keep the peace.
It's okay to say "no."
It's okay to rest.
It's okay to ask for more.

I'd tell you that your softness is not a flaw.
That your emotions are not too much.
That one day, your empathy will be your superpower—
not your burden.

And most of all, I'd say this:
You are deeply, wildly, beautifully worthy—
even when no one sees it yet.

Love,
Me (But stronger, softer, freer)

**Morning Reflection:**

The boy you once were still lives inside you — waiting to be heard, seen, loved.

**Prompt:**

- **Write a letter to your younger self. What does he need to know today?**

_____
_____
_____
_____
_____
_____
_____
_____

**Mindful Minute:**

Visualize that younger version of you. Hold his hand. Breathe with him.

**Mantra:**

*I honor the boy I was and the man I am becoming.*

**Evening Reflection:**

- Did I show up for my inner child today?

_____
_____
_____
_____
_____
_____
_____
_____

# DAY 300: Letters Left Unread

Some letters were never meant to be sent.
Words that once burned on the tongue
found their resting place in quiet journals,
folded beneath years of growth and silence.

Letters to those who left without explanation.
To those who stayed, but never truly saw you.
To the version of yourself who didn't know better—
or didn't feel allowed to want more.

These letters hold truths I couldn't say out loud.
Not because they weren't valid,
but because sometimes healing happens
without confrontation.

They were my release.
My reclamation.
My way of telling the truth
without needing it to be received.

Not every chapter needs an audience.
Not every feeling needs a reply.
Sometimes, closure is quiet.
Sometimes, healing is choosing peace
over permission.

And in those letters left unread—
I found my voice.
I found my self-respect.
And that was enough.

## Morning Reflection:

There will always be things we wish we'd said. But not every letter needs a reply.

**Prompt:**

- **What closure are you seeking from someone who may never respond?**

_____
_____
_____
_____
_____
_____
_____

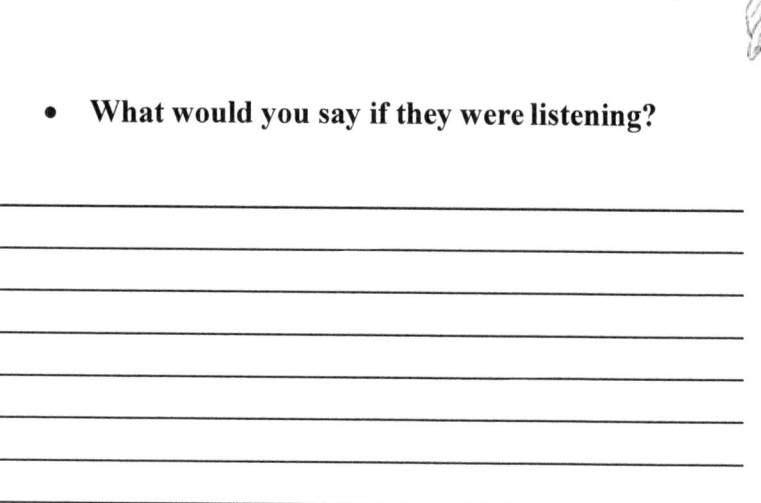

- **What would you say if they were listening?**

_____
_____
_____
_____
_____
_____
_____
_____

## Mindful Minute:

Release the need for reply. Feel the lightness of expression for its own sake.

## Mantra:

*I let go without needing anything back.*

**Evening Reflection:**

- **What freedom did I find in letting go?**

_____
_____
_____
_____
_____
_____
_____
_____

# DAY 301: The Letter I'll Live By

Dear Me,
You don't need anyone's permission to be whole.
Not another achievement.
Not another apology.
Not another round of proving you're worthy.

You were always enough — before the striving,
before the masks,
before the weight of other people's expectations
started feeling like your own.

This letter isn't to change you.
It's to remind you.
That softness isn't weakness.
That presence is powerful.
That rest is not earned — it's yours by right.

You don't have to hustle for belonging.
You already belong — to the ground beneath your feet,
to the breath in your lungs,
to the love you give and receive.

Live gently.
Speak kindly — especially to yourself.
Laugh without shrinking.

Grieve without guilt.
Dream without apology.

Let this be your compass:
You are allowed to begin again.
To rest.
To say no.
To say yes to the life that calls to you
even if no one else hears it.

This is your letter.
Not written to be folded away,
but to be lived,
out loud.

**Morning Reflection:**

When the writing ends, the living begins. Let your truth shape how you move forward.

**Prompt:**

- **Write yourself a manifesto — a commitment to how you'll live from now on. Keep it honest. Keep it bold.**

_____
_____
_____
_____
_____
_____
_____
_____

**Mindful Minute:**

Read your words aloud. Let them resonate in your body.

**Mantra:**

*I live by my truth — not just my survival.*

**Evening Reflection:**

- Did my actions align with the letter I wrote to myself?

_____
_____
_____
_____
_____
_____
_____

# WEEK 44 — Returning Home to Myself

"Your body is your home. Your heart is your compass. Your truth is your path."

This week is about coming home — not to a place, but to yourself. After months of reflection, growth, and letting go, it's time to reclaim your wholeness. No more chasing approval. No more hiding parts of yourself. You belong — fully, here.

# DAY 302 : The Man I Am

I am not the echoes of other people's expectations.
I am not the roles I was handed without consent —
protector, provider, performer.

I am the man who is learning to breathe first,
before holding up the world.
The man who is soft where he once hardened.
Curious where he once felt shame.

I am the man who now knows that vulnerability
isn't something to overcome —
it's something to honor.

The man who no longer apologizes
for needing rest,
for asking questions,
for feeling deeply.

I am the man who sits with his fears
without letting them define him.
The man who can listen without fixing,
and cry without explanation.

I am becoming —
not by becoming someone else,
but by returning to myself.
Over and over.
With grace.


This is the man I am:
Still healing.
Still growing.
Still worthy.
Just as I am

**Morning Reflection:**

Take a moment to see yourself as you are today — not your past, not your projections — but the man here, now.

**Prompt:**

- Who am I today?

_____
_____
_____
_____
_____
_____
_____

- What do I know about myself now that I didn't before?

_____
_____
_____
_____
_____
_____
_____

**Mindful Minute:**

Stand in front of a mirror. Look into your own eyes and say, "Welcome home."

### Mantra:

*I am not becoming. I already am.*

**Evening Reflection:**

- **Did I see myself clearly today — without judgment?**

_____
_____
_____
_____
_____
_____
_____

## DAY 303: Where I Belong

Belonging was once a place I searched for —
in people, performance, and approval.
I chased it in rooms where I had to shrink,
in conversations where my truth stayed silent.

But now, I understand:
Belonging isn't found in fitting in.
It's found in standing true.

I belong where I can be all of me —
not just the strong parts,
not just the calm exterior,
but the full spectrum:
the soft, the unsure, the growing.

I belong in spaces that honor complexity,
where questions are welcome
and masks aren't required.

I belong in my own presence,
on my own path,
in my own timing.

Because when I stop performing to be accepted,
when I stop hiding to feel loved —
I find that I belong wherever I bring my whole self.

And that is enough.
I am enough.
Here. Now.
Fully.
Finally.
Home.

**Morning Reflection:**

True belonging isn't about fitting in. It's about being fully yourself in the world — and still knowing you are worthy of love.

**Prompt:**

- **When do I feel most at home in my skin?**

_____
_____
_____
_____
_____
_____
_____
_____

- **What moments bring me peace?**

_____
_____
_____
_____
_____

### Mindful Minute:

Close your eyes. Visualize a place, memory, or feeling that feels like "home." Stay there.

### Mantra:

*I belong to myself first.*

**Evening Reflection:**

- **Where did I feel safe being fully me today?**

_____
_____
_____
_____
_____
_____
_____

# DAY 304: Safe Inside My Skin

For so long, my body felt like a battlefield—
a place I braced against,
tightened up,
escaped from.

I learned to carry tension like armor,
to move like I was always under threat,
to exist as though I needed permission
to rest, breathe, just be.

But something is shifting.
Now, I am learning to stay.
To feel.
To listen.

I am slowly making peace
with the rise and fall of my breath,
the curve of my back,
the way my shoulders lower
when I finally stop pretending to be okay.

My body is not a problem to fix.
It is a home to return to.
A compass.
A vessel of memory and resilience.

Today, I remind myself:
I don't need to outrun my feelings.
I don't need to perform safety.
I am allowed to feel safe—
here, inside my skin.

And even if it's unfamiliar,
even if it takes time,
I will keep coming back
until "safe" feels like me.

**Morning Reflection:**

Coming home means finding safety within your own body, emotions, and presence — even when the world is loud.

**Prompt:**

- **What makes me feel safe inside myself? How can I protect and nurture that?**

_____
_____
_____
_____
_____
_____
_____

**Mindful Minute:**

Wrap your arms around yourself. Inhale peace. Exhale anxiety.

**Mantra:**

*I am safe within me.*

**Evening Reflection:**

- **Did I feel grounded and at peace in my body today?**

_____
_____
_____
_____
_____
_____
_____
_____

# Month 10 Reflection: Gratitude + Grief

1. **What I'm Grateful For That I Didn't Expect**

- **Name a surprise gift, person, lesson, or moment.**

_____
_____
_____
_____
_____
_____
_____
_____

# DAY 305 — Reclaiming My Narrative

For years, I lived inside a story that wasn't mine.
A version of me shaped by expectations,
by silence,
by survival.

I learned how to be agreeable,
to say the right things,
to shrink myself into spaces
that were never meant to hold all of me.

I mistook approval for truth,
and performance for identity.

But now—
I am taking the pen back.

Not to rewrite the past,
but to *own* it.
To trace the wounds *and* the wisdom.
To name what happened,
what I lost,
what I found along the way.

This is not about erasing chapters—
it's about remembering
that the story isn't over.

Every word I speak in my own voice,
every boundary I set,
every truth I tell—
they all become part of the new story
I'm writing for myself.

One rooted not in shame or proving,
but in freedom,
dignity,
and belonging.

This is my narrative now.
And I choose to live it fully.

**Morning Reflection:**

You are not your mistakes. You are not just your survival story. You are the author of what comes next.

**Prompt:**

- **What parts of my story do I need to reclaim, reframe, or own with pride?**

_____
_____
_____
_____
_____
_____
_____

**Mindful Minute:**

Whisper: "My story is mine to tell." Repeat until it resonates.

**Mantra:**

*I am the author of my life.*

**Evening Reflection:**

- Did I honor my past without letting it define my present?

_____
_____
_____
_____
_____
_____
_____
_____

# DAY 306 — Living Without Permission

For too long, I waited.
Waited for approval.
For validation.
For someone to say,
"Yes, you can live as *you*."

I shrunk my voice,
dimmed my light,
postponed my becoming—
because I thought I needed a green light
from someone else's comfort.

But permission was never theirs to give.

I don't need to justify my dreams
or dilute my truth
to fit into someone else's idea
of what's "right" or "acceptable."

Living without permission means
I no longer apologize for my presence.
It means I stop outsourcing my worth.
It means I dare to live boldly,
messily,
authentically.

Some will misunderstand.
Some will walk away.

But what I gain—
is me.

This is the life I get.
And I'm done waiting
for someone else
to let me live it.

**Morning Reflection:**

You don't need anyone's permission to live boldly, fully, and freely. You already have it — from yourself.

**Prompt:**

- **Where have I been waiting for permission?**

_____
_____
_____
_____
_____
_____
_____

- **What would change if I stopped waiting?**

　　_____
　　_____
　　_____
　　_____
　　_____
　　_____
　　_____
　　_____

### Mindful Minute:

Inhale confidence. Exhale hesitation.

### Mantra:

*I give myself full permission to live.*

**Evening Reflection:**

- **Where did I move freely today?**

_____
_____
_____
_____
_____
_____
_____

# DAY 307: My Peace, My Priority

There was a time when I bent in every direction
just to keep the peace—
but never mine.

I over-explained,
over-functioned,
over-committed,
and under-protected my own soul.

Now, I've learned:
peace isn't passive.
It's not the absence of conflict—
it's the presence of alignment.
And it begins with me.

My peace is no longer a luxury.
It's a boundary.
A choice.
A compass.

I don't owe anyone access
that costs me my calm.
I don't have to stay in spaces
where I constantly have to shrink to fit.

I am allowed to pause.
To step back.
To not respond.
To guard the quiet I've worked so hard to cultivate.

Because at the end of the day,
if I'm not at peace—
nothing else is truly worth it.

So I return to my center,
reclaim my breath,
and remind myself:


**My peace is not negotiable.**

### Morning Reflection:

Peace is not found — it is chosen, protected, and prioritized every day.

**Prompt:**

- **What threatens my peace?**

_____
_____
_____
_____
_____
_____
_____

- **What protects it?**

_____
_____
_____
_____
_____
_____
_____

**Mindful Minute:**

Breathe in clarity. Breathe out the noise.

### Mantra:

*My peace is my daily commitment.*

**Evening Reflection:**

- **What did I say "no" to today in order to protect my peace?**

_____
_____
_____
_____
_____
_____
_____
_____

# DAY 308: Home Is Me

For so long, I searched for home
in people, places, and approval.
I tried to earn it with performance,
maintain it through perfection,
and chase it in the comfort of the familiar.

But eventually, I learned—
home is not a destination.
It's not found in the arms of another
or in the echo of someone else's validation.

**Home is me.**

It's the steadiness I build within.
The safety I offer myself
when the world feels unsteady.
The soft place I return to
when the day has taken more than it gave.

I am the place I get to exhale.
The space where all versions of me
—tired, joyful, unsure, healing—
are allowed to exist without performance.

I carry home in the way I speak to myself,
in how I protect my peace,
in how I trust my own belonging.

No more searching for shelter in broken places.
No more abandoning myself to be chosen.

Today, I come home.
And I stay.
Because **I am home.**
And that is enough.

**Morning Reflection:**

This is the week's truth: You are your own home. Wherever you go, you carry yourself. Make it a place of love.

**Prompt:**

- **What does "being at home in myself" mean?**

_____
_____
_____
_____
_____
_____
_____
_____

- **How do I live that daily?**

_____
_____
_____
_____
_____
_____
_____
_____
_____

### Mindful Minute:

Place one hand on your chest and one on your belly. Breathe. Feel yourself.

### Mantra:

*I am home. I am whole. I am here.*

**Evening Reflection:**

- Did I come home to myself today — even in the smallest ways?

_____
_____
_____
_____
_____
_____
_____

# WEEK 45 — Love, Actually

"Love isn't a reward. It's your birthright."

This week, we strip love of the performance, fear, and perfectionism we've layered on it. Love is not what we earn — it's what we are. This chapter invites you to receive it, give it, and most importantly, live it.

# DAY 309: Letting Love In

It's easier sometimes to give than to receive.
To pour out kindness, affirmation, service—
while quietly refusing the same in return.
Because love that comes *in*
requires openness,
vulnerability,
a softening of the walls I've spent years building.

Letting love in means believing
I am worthy of it,
not because of what I do,
but because of who I am.
It means trusting that tenderness
won't be used against me,
that affection doesn't come
with hidden expectations.

I've been the strong one.
The one who helps, holds, and hides.
But strength can also look like
open hands,
wet eyes,
and saying, "Yes, I could use some love today."

Today, I practice receiving.
A compliment without deflection.

Support without guilt.
Care without suspicion.
Love, in all its honest and quiet forms.

Because I am not just a giver of love—
I am worthy of it too.
And now, finally,
I am letting it in.

## Morning Reflection:

Many of us know how to give love — but struggle to receive it. What if you let it in today?

**Prompt:**

- **Where have I been closing the door on love — and why?**

_____
_____
_____
_____
_____
_____
_____

## Mindful Minute:

Place your palm over your heart and breathe in this truth: "I am worthy of love."

## Mantra:

*I let love in — without resistance.*

**Evening Reflection:**

- **Did I allow myself to be loved today?**

_____
_____
_____
_____
_____
_____
_____

# DAY 310: Love Without Armor

For so long, I thought I had to protect love—
to guard it with logic,
to keep it neat,
to never need too much
or show too much
or hope too deeply.

I wore my armor into every connection:
over-explaining,
bracing for rejection,
keeping things safe and shallow
so I wouldn't feel exposed.

But love can't breathe under armor.
It needs soft spaces.
It needs unguarded moments,
where the truth of who I am
can meet the truth of who you are.

Love without armor is risky.
It might ache.
It might change me.
But it also frees me.
Because when I stop performing strength,
I become available to real connection—

not just being admired,
but being known.

So today, I let love in
without filters,
without the mask of "I'm fine,"
without the story that I need to earn it.

I am learning to love and be loved
not with my fists clenched,
but with my arms open.
No armor.
Just me.
And that's enough.

**Morning Reflection:**

Love without vulnerability isn't love. It's performance.
Today, risk being seen.

**Prompt:**

- **Where do I hide in love?**

_____
_____
_____
_____
_____
_____

- **Who do I pretend to be?**

_____
_____
_____
_____
_____
_____

**Mindful Minute:**

Breathe with your shoulders relaxed and heart open.
Imagine your defenses dissolving.

**Mantra:**

*I love bravely, not perfectly.*

**Evening Reflection:**

- Where did I show up as my full self in love today?

_____
_____
_____
_____
_____
_____
_____

# DAY 311: I Am Lovable

I used to think love had to be earned—
through achievement,
through selflessness,
through staying quiet
when I wanted to speak.

I measured my worth
by how useful I was,
how agreeable I seemed,
how well I could disappear
to keep the peace.

But I'm unlearning that now.
I am not lovable *because* I perform,
because I don't need much,
or because I always get it right.

I am lovable
because I exist.
Because my presence matters.
Because my heart beats,
and it longs,
and it hopes.

I am lovable
even when I'm not perfect,

even when I'm healing,
even when I feel unsure.

I don't have to shrink for love.
I don't have to strive for it.
I don't have to beg for it.

I get to *receive* it.
Fully. Freely. Fiercely.
As I am.
Right here.
Right now.

Today, I remind myself—
I am lovable.
And nothing can take that away.

**Morning Reflection:**

Let this be a declaration: I am lovable. Not when I'm fixed.
Not when I'm better. Now.

**Prompt:**

- **What stories have I told myself about not being lovable?**

_____
_____
_____
_____
_____
_____
_____

- **Are they true?**

_____
_____
_____
_____
_____
_____
_____

**Mindful Minute:**

Whisper this: "I am lovable just as I am." Three times. Out loud.

**Mantra:**

*I am worthy of love today, not someday.*

**Evening Reflection:**

- **Did I treat myself with the love I want from others?**

_____
_____
_____
_____
_____
_____
_____

# DAY 312: Love Is Not a Transaction

For too long, I believed love was something I had to earn.
That if I gave enough, fixed enough, proved enough,
then I'd be worthy of being kept.
That love was a trade —
my effort for someone's attention,
my silence for someone's comfort,
my self-abandonment for someone's approval.

But that's not love.
That's survival.

Real love isn't measured by how much I do,
but by how much I am allowed to be.
It doesn't tally debts or keep score.
It doesn't say, *"Only if..."*
It says, *"Even now."*

Love doesn't demand my exhaustion.
It doesn't ask me to disappear.

Today, I release the idea
that I have to perform to be loved.
I stop auditioning for belonging.

Love is not a transaction —
it's a presence.
It's choosing, not chasing.
It's safety, not sacrifice.

I am worthy of the kind of love
that doesn't keep receipts.
And I am learning to give it to myself first.

**Morning Reflection:**

If you have to earn it, it's not love. That's survival. Real love holds space, not scorecards.

**Prompt:**

- **Where have I confused love with approval, attention, or obligation?**

**Mindful Minute:**

Sit still and breathe in this truth: "I do not have to perform for love."

**Mantra:**

*I choose love that frees, not love that traps.*

**Evening Reflection:**

- **Did I practice unconditional love today — for myself or someone else?**

_____
_____
_____
_____
_____
_____
_____

# DAY 313 — Loving From Overflow

### Morning Reflection:

You can't pour love from an empty cup. Fill yours first — not as selfishness, but as service.

### Prompt:

- **How can I love from a place of wholeness today?**

_____
_____
_____
_____
_____
_____
_____

### Mindful Minute:

Breathe deeply. On each exhale, release the pressure to do more than you can.

## Mantra:

*I love from overflow, not depletion.*

**Evening Reflection:**

- **Was I grounded in love today — or drained?**

_____
_____
_____
_____
_____
_____
_____
_____

## DAY 314 : Love Is a Daily Practice

Love isn't a grand gesture.
It's not a milestone to reach or a finish line to cross.
It's the quiet choice I make — over and over again.

To show up.
To listen.
To forgive.
To be honest, even when it's hard.
To soften when everything in me wants to shut down.
To be present, even when I'm tired.

Love is in how I speak to myself when I mess up.
It's in how I hold space for the people I care about.
It's in how I don't run when things get uncomfortable.

Love is less about how loud I say it
and more about how consistently I live it.

Today, I remember that love is not just a feeling —
it's a practice.
A rhythm.
A discipline of the heart.
It asks for patience.
It invites presence.
And it begins with how I treat myself.

I don't have to get it perfect.
I just have to keep showing up.

With gentleness. With courage.
With love. Every day.

### Morning Reflection:

Love is more verb than feeling. It's built in the ordinary — in kindness, honesty, and care.

### Prompt:

- **How can I show up in love today — even in small, unglamorous ways?**

_____
_____
_____
_____
_____
_____
_____

**Mindful Minute:**

Bring to mind one person you love. Send them warmth and peace in your breath.

**Mantra:**

*Today, I choose to love well.*

**Evening Reflection:**

- **Where did I make love real today?**

_____
_____
_____
_____
_____
_____
_____

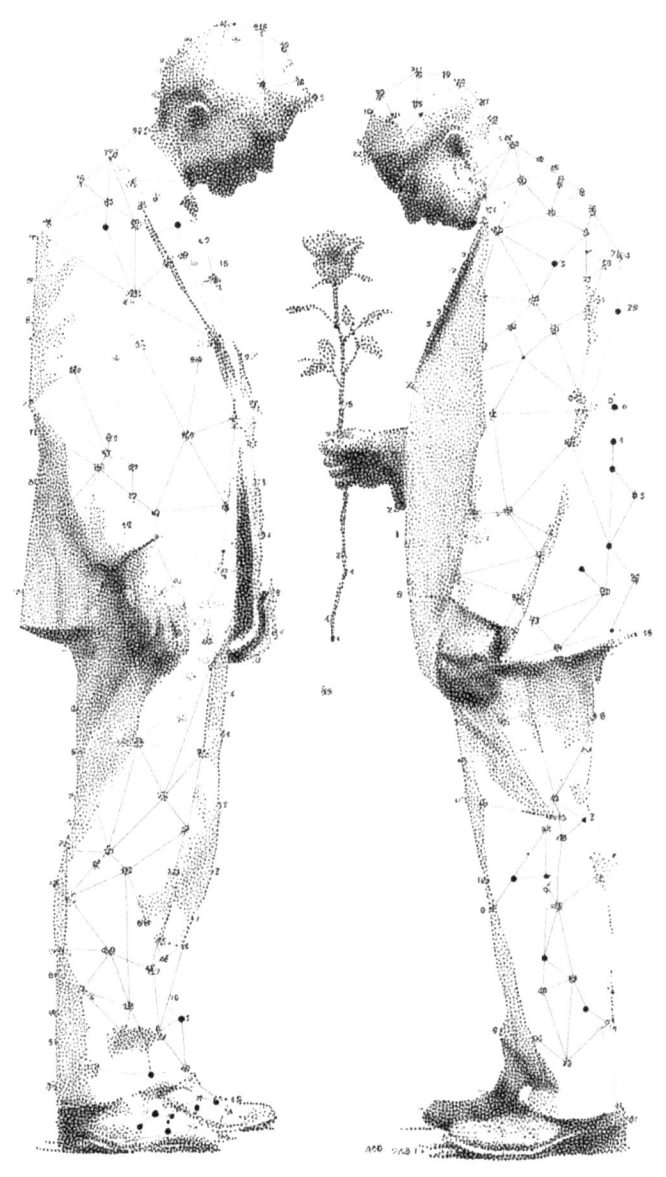

# DAY 315: Love Starts Here

Before it reaches anyone else —
before it fills a room,
builds a bond,
or changes the world —
love has to begin *within me*.

Not the love that performs.
Not the love that chases validation.
Not the love that waits for permission.

But the love that's rooted.
The kind that knows:
**I am worthy.**
**I am enough.**
**I am lovable — now.**

Love starts here,
in the way I hold myself when I'm hurting.
In the way I speak gently when I could criticize.
In the way I choose rest instead of running on empty.
In the way I stop abandoning myself for acceptance.

The world taught me to give love away first.
To earn it. To prove it.
But healing has taught me to plant it at home —
in my chest,

in my choices,
in my breath.

Today, I don't wait for love to come from out there.
I choose it in here.
In the mirror.
In my mind.
In my heartbeat.

Love starts here.
And from here, it overflows.

### Morning Reflection:

Before love becomes a connection to others, it must become a sanctuary in you. This is where it starts.

**Prompt:**

- What would it look like to root my life in love — not fear?

_____
_____
_____
_____
_____
_____
_____
_____

**Mindful Minute:**

Sit with your breath. Let it be soft, loving, and full.

**Mantra:**

*I am love, already.*

**Evening Reflection:**

- Did I live as love today — in my thoughts, actions, and choices?

_____
_____
_____
_____
_____
_____
_____

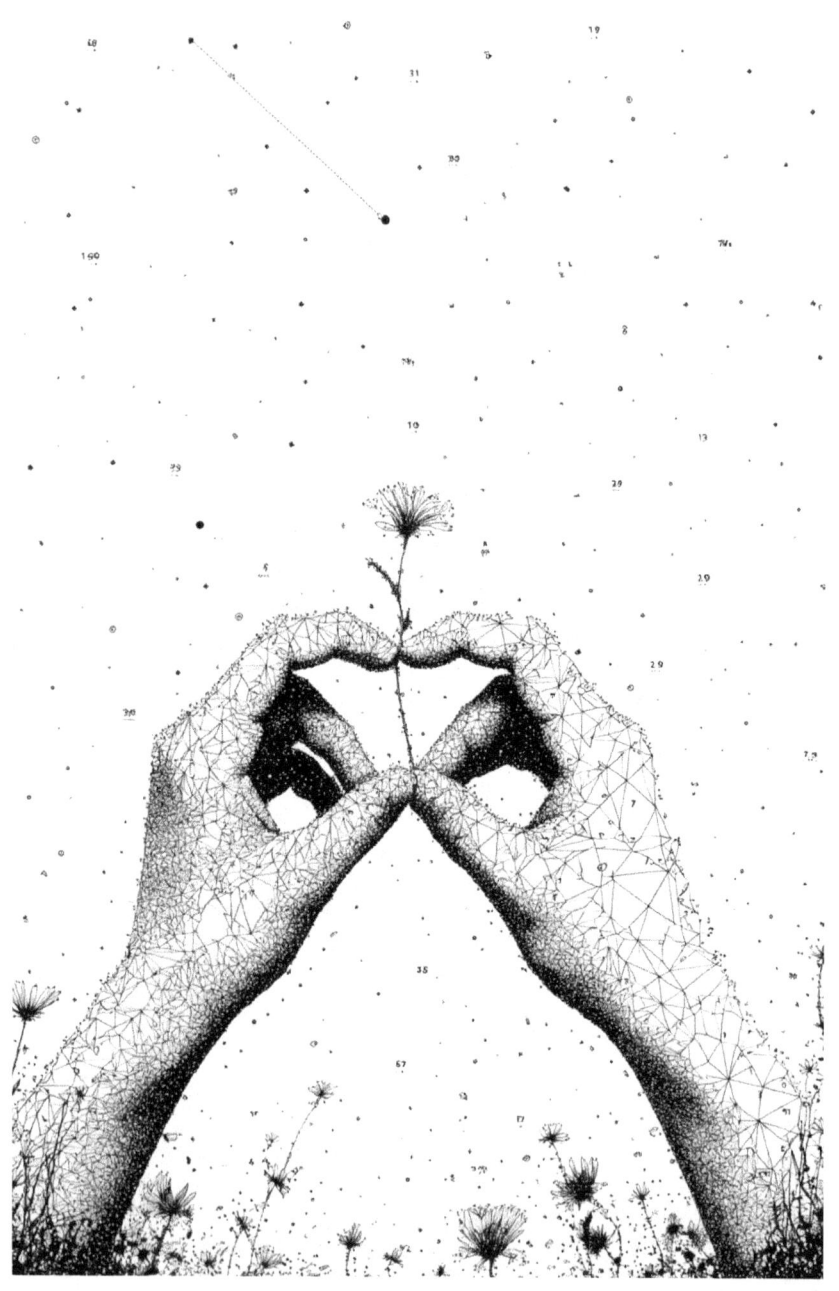

# WEEK 46 — Spiritual Integrity

"Let your beliefs meet your behavior — that's where peace lives."

This week is a sacred alignment. We explore what it means to **live** our truth, not just believe it. Spiritual integrity is not perfection — it's authenticity. It's when who you say you are and how you move through the world start speaking the same language.

# DAY 316: What Do I Believe?

When the noise quiets
and the performances fall away,
what do I *really* believe?

About love.
About healing.
About strength.
About *me*?

I've been handed beliefs —
from culture, family, religion, pain —
some I wore like armor,
others like chains.
Some helped me survive,
others made me shrink.

But I'm allowed to re-examine.
To unlearn.
To ask again.

Do I believe that rest is weakness?
That love must be earned?
That emotions are a threat?
That vulnerability makes me less?

Or…
Do I believe in softness with power,

in presence over performance,
in love that doesn't

**Morning Reflection:**

- What do I truly believe about life, love, purpose, and myself — when no one's watching?

_____
_____
_____
_____
_____
_____
_____

**Prompt:**

- If I stripped away every inherited belief, what would I still hold onto?

_____
_____
_____
_____
_____
_____
_____

**Mindful Minute:**

Close your eyes and say: "I welcome my own truth." Listen to what arises.

**Mantra:**

*My truth is sacred and evolving.*

**Evening Reflection:**

- **Did I live in alignment with my real values today?**

_____
_____
_____
_____
_____
_____
_____
_____

# DAY 317: When Belief Becomes Behavior

What I believe shapes how I behave —
even when I'm not aware of it.

If I believe I'm not worthy,
I might shrink in conversations.
If I believe emotions are dangerous,
I might suppress what's real.
If I believe I always have to be strong,
I might never ask for help.

Beliefs are like roots.
Behaviors are the branches.
I can trim and correct the outer growth,
but true change begins underground.

So today, I pause and ask:
Where did this behavior start?
What belief is feeding it?
And do I still choose to believe that?

I can replant new truths.
I can nurture better roots

## Morning Reflection:

It's easy to believe in compassion. Harder to live it when triggered. Integrity is the bridge.

## Prompt:

- **Where does my behavior contradict what I say I value?**

_____
_____
_____
_____
_____
_____
_____

## Mindful Minute:

Think of one value that matters deeply to you. Breathe into that word.

**Mantra:**

*I practice what I preach — with grace.*

**Evening Reflection:**

- **Where did I close the gap between my words and actions?**

_____
_____
_____
_____
_____
_____
_____

# DAY 318: Sacred, Not Spectacle

I'm learning
to keep some moments just for me —
the quiet victories,
the silent releases,
the private reconciliations
between who I was
and who I'm becoming.

I don't owe the world my process
in real-time.
I can protect the parts of me
that are still tender,
still forming,
still learning to trust.

Not because I'm hiding—
but because some things are holy.

My healing doesn't need validation
to be valid.
My peace doesn't need performance
to be powerful.

Some things are sacred.
And that is enough.

## Morning Reflection:

Your spiritual life is not a performance. It's private, personal, and precious.

### Prompt:

- **Am I more focused on being seen as "spiritual" than on living with soul?**

_____
_____
_____
_____
_____
_____
_____

## Mindful Minute:

Place your hand over your heart. Whisper: "This is my sanctuary."

## Mantra:

*I honor what's sacred — even in silence.*

**Evening Reflection:**

- **Did I ground my day in spirit — not spectacle?**

_____
_____
_____
_____
_____
_____
_____
_____

# DAY 319: Your Life Is Your Message

Not your title.
Not your résumé.
Not the curated posts.
Not the highlight reel.

But how you move through the world.
How you listen when someone speaks.
How you show up when no one is watching.
How you treat the people
who can't offer you anything in return.

Your life is your message.
The quiet choices.
The unseen kindness.
The steady presence.
The healing you've done in silence
that now spills gently into how you love.

You don't need a microphone
to make an impact.
You don't need a platform
to live with purpose.

Every breath,
every boundary,
every act of courage
is a note in the song of your becoming.

Let it be honest.
Let it be kind.
Let it be true.
Because you—
just living in your fullness—
is already a message worth hearing.

**Morning Reflection:**

You don't need a platform to be impactful. Integrity speaks volumes — even quietly.

**Prompt:**

- **What is my life preaching to others?**

_____
_____
_____
_____
_____
_____
_____
_____

### Mindful Minute:

Inhale honesty. Exhale alignment. Feel the peace of consistency.

### Mantra:

*May my life speak love, even when I say nothing.*

**Evening Reflection:**

- Did my actions reflect the message I want to leave in this world?

_____
_____
_____
_____
_____
_____
_____

# DAY 320: Don't Weaponize Your Wisdom

You've healed.
You've grown.
You've done the work.
But don't let that work become a weapon.

Wisdom isn't a ladder to look down from.
It's not a tool for shaming those
still finding their way.
It's a light—
meant to illuminate,
not to blind.

Sometimes, the deeper we go,
the easier it becomes
to forget how it felt to be lost.
But grace remembers.
Grace speaks with gentleness.
It holds space for the version of you
who didn't know better yet.

You're not here to correct everyone.
You're not here to prove your evolution.
You're here to live your truth—
humbly, honestly,
without the need to convert or convince.

Let your wisdom be an invitation,
not a judgement.
Let your presence remind people
what is possible—
not what they've failed to become.

True wisdom knows when to speak.
And just as importantly,
when to simply sit beside someone
in quiet understanding.

### Morning Reflection:

Spirituality can heal — or it can harm when used to shame, control, or manipulate. Let's choose healing.

**Prompt:**

- **Have I ever used my beliefs to elevate myself or diminish others?**

_____
_____
_____
_____
_____
_____

### Mindful Minute:

Breathe in humility. Let it settle in your body like calm truth.

### Mantra:

*I use my truth to heal, not to harm.*

### Evening Reflection:

- **Where did I show grace to someone on a different path today?**

_____
_____
_____
_____
_____
_____
_____
_____

# DAY 321: Permission to Evolve

You don't have to be who you were.
Not yesterday.
Not five years ago.
Not in the stories others still tell about you.

You are allowed to grow.
To shift.
To outgrow containers
that once felt like home.

This is your permission slip—
to release outdated expectations,
to unlearn habits rooted in survival,
to say, "That version of me served a purpose…
but it's not who I am today."

You are not a static image.
You are movement.
You are motion.
You are becoming.

Let them be surprised.
Let them misunderstand.
Let them call it inconsistency.
You call it growth.

You were never meant to be a statue—
you were meant to bloom,

shed,
transform.

And in the process,
you give others permission too.
To evolve.
To reintroduce themselves.
To live into the truth of who they're becoming—
not who they were told to be.

## Morning Reflection:

You are allowed to change — your beliefs, your path, your understanding. Growth is holy.

**Prompt:**

- **What belief or spiritual practice have I outgrown?**

_____
_____
_____
_____
_____
_____
_____

### Mindful Minute:

As you inhale, repeat: "I am growing." As you exhale: "And that is sacred."

### Mantra:

*I evolve with courage and clarity.*

**Evening Reflection:**

- **Did I allow space for growth and new understanding today?**

_____
_____
_____
_____
_____
_____
_____
_____

# DAY 322: The Integrity of Rest

Rest is not avoidance.
It is not weakness.
It is not a reward reserved for when you've "earned it."

Rest is integrity.
Because to rest is to tell the truth—
about your limits,
about your needs,
about your humanity.

In a world that glorifies burnout,
rest becomes an act of courage.
A quiet rebellion that says:
"I will not abandon myself for the sake of appearing strong."

There is nothing lazy about honoring your body. There is nothing shameful about stepping away. There is deep honesty in saying:
"I need time. I need stillness. I need space."

Rest isn't a pause from real life—
it is part of real life.
It sustains you.
It roots you.
It reminds you that you are not a machine.

And when you honor rest,
you teach others to honor it too.
You create a culture where breath is not a luxury—
but a right.

So today, rest without apology.
Without guilt.
Without the need to prove your worth.

Your value is not in what you produce.
Your integrity is in how well you care for what's within.

## Morning Reflection:

Sometimes the most spiritual thing you can do is stop.
Breathe. Be. That is enough.

**Prompt:**

- **Where have I equated hustle with holiness?**

_____
_____
_____
_____
_____
_____
_____

**Mindful Minute:**

Sit in silence for one minute. Let stillness be your devotion.

**Mantra:**

*Rest is holy. I honor it.*

**Evening Reflection:**

- **Did I allow rest to be part of my spiritual rhythm today?**

_____
_____
_____
_____
_____
_____
_____

# WEEK 47 — Joyful Masculinity

*"Real masculinity is not a burden. It's a blessing — when lived with joy."*

This week reclaims *masculinity* as a vibrant, healing, and expressive force. Joyful masculinity isn't about dominance — it's about being *whole*. Play, tenderness, presence, laughter, strength — all of it belongs.

## DAY 323: Permission to Be Soft

You don't have to harden to survive.
You don't have to carry sharp edges to prove you're strong.
You don't need to tuck away tenderness to be respected.

Softness is not the absence of strength—
It's the presence of wholeness.

We were never meant to be only one thing.
Only tough.
Only unshaken.
Only composed.

There is power in being gentle with yourself.
There is courage in letting your emotions be visible.
There is strength in choosing compassion over control.

Being soft doesn't mean you don't feel pain—
It means you've stopped fighting yourself to hide it.

It means you can meet life with open hands,
Even when you're unsure.
Even when you're healing.
Even when you're growing.

So if no one has told you:
You have permission to be soft.

To cry.
To care deeply.
To hold instead of fix.
To pause instead of push.

You are still whole.
Still worthy.
Still strong.

Softness isn't the opposite of power—
It's where power learns to breathe

**Morning Reflection:**

Masculinity doesn't require hardness. Your softness is not weakness — it's wisdom.

**Prompt:**

- What part of me have I suppressed to appear "strong"?

_____
_____
_____
_____
_____
_____
_____

**Mindful Minute:**

Place your palm on your chest. Breathe. Say: "I am safe to be soft."

**Mantra:**

*I make space for tenderness.*

**Evening Reflection:**

- Did I show up today with softness — to myself or others?

_____
_____
_____
_____
_____
_____
_____

# DAY 324: Redefining Strength

Strength is not just what lifts, carries, or endures.
It's what bends without breaking.
What listens when it could shout.
What stays when it would be easier to run.

The old definitions taught us that strength meant silence,
control,
suppression,
stoicism at all costs.
But those were borrowed beliefs—
handed down through generations of fear
and survival, not truth.

Today, strength looks different.

It's the willingness to say "I don't know."
It's the ability to rest without guilt.
It's the bravery to ask for help
and the courage to accept love without earning it.

Real strength is gentle hands holding grief.
It's a trembling voice telling the truth.
It's showing up fully—cracks, scars, stories and all.

The strongest people I know cry without apology,
love without armor,
and live without pretending.

So maybe it's time we retire the old script—
the one that said we had to be tough to be worthy.
Because the new strength—
the real kind—
is rooted in honesty,
softness,
and the freedom to be fully human.

You don't have to break to prove you're unbreakable.
You don't have to harden to prove you're strong.

**Morning Reflection:**

Real strength isn't just muscle or stoicism. It's emotional bravery. It's crying and trying again.

**Prompt:**

- **How do I define strength today?**

_____
_____
_____
_____
_____
_____
_____
_____

- **What needs redefining?**

_____
_____
_____
_____
_____
_____
_____
_____

**Mindful Minute:**

Flex your hands. Now relax them. Feel the power in ease.

**Mantra:**

*My strength is soulful, not showy.*

**Evening Reflection:**

- **Where did I show real strength — the vulnerable kind?**

_____
_____
_____
_____
_____
_____
_____
_____

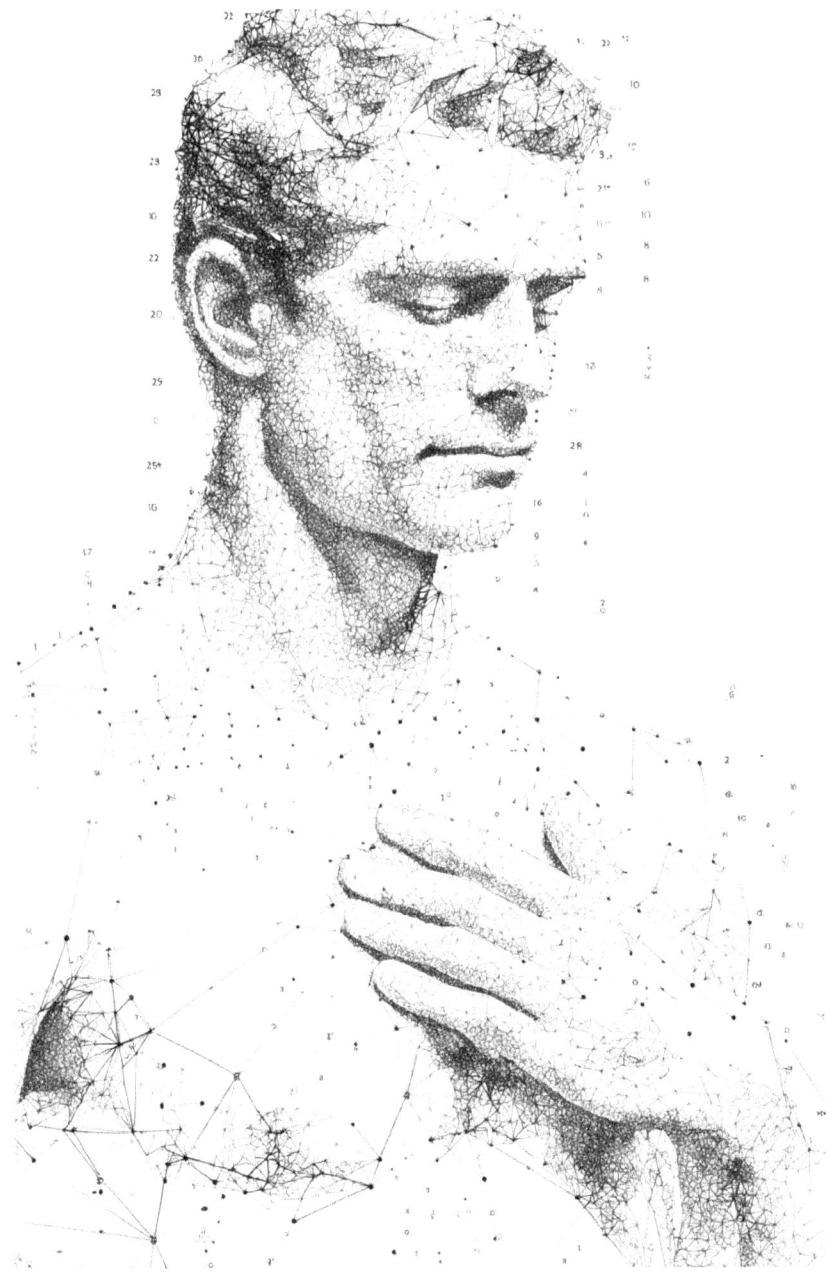

# DAY 325: The Joy of Brotherhood

There's a kind of healing that only happens
in the company of those who see you without judgment—
who laugh with you, cry with you,
and sit in silence when words fall short.

Brotherhood is not built on bravado
or shared performance of strength.
It's built on presence, honesty, and witness.
On checking in—really checking in.
On the unspoken nods,
the safe space to unravel,
and the shared permission to be human.

In a world that often tells men to isolate,
to compete, to mask—
brotherhood says:
"You don't have to carry it alone."

There is joy in that kind of knowing.
Joy in the shared stories,
the lifted burdens,
the belly laughs after long days.
Joy in someone remembering your quiet battles
and showing up anyway.

Brotherhood doesn't demand perfection.
It invites truth.
It celebrates the man you are becoming,
while honoring the path you've walked.

And when the world gets loud,
when you're tempted to disappear into your struggle—
a brother reminds you:
You're not alone. You never were.
And that's a joy worth holding onto.

## Morning Reflection:

Healthy male friendships heal generations. Brotherhood isn't weakness — it's legacy.

**Prompt:**

- **Who are the men I feel safe with?**

_____
_____
_____
_____
_____
_____
_____

- **Have I thanked them lately?**

_____
_____
_____
_____
_____
_____
_____

## Mindful Minute:

Think of a friend or brother you love. Send them silent gratitude.

**Mantra:**

*Brotherhood builds me.*

**Evening Reflection:**

- **How did I nurture connection with another man today?**

_____
_____
_____
_____
_____
_____
_____
_____
_____

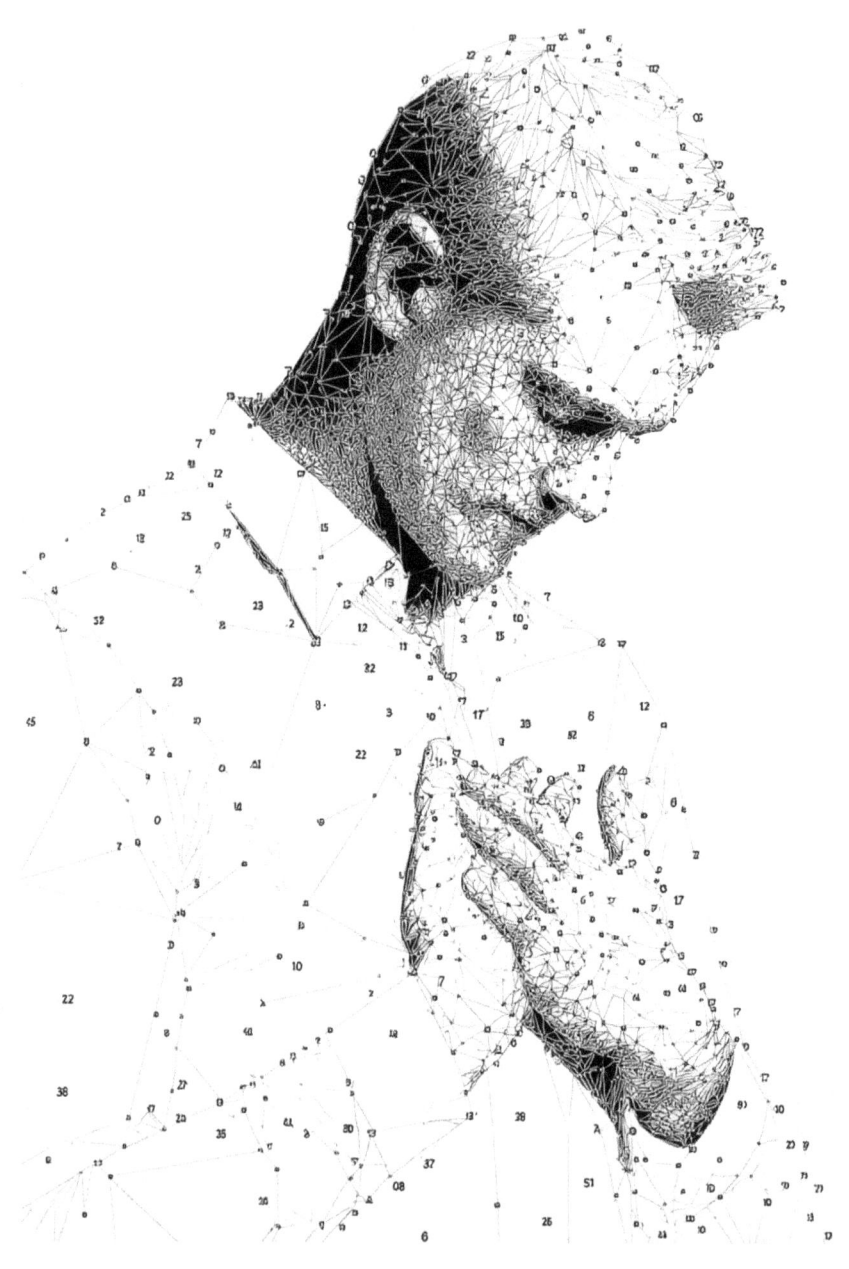

# DAY 326: Play Is Power

Somewhere along the way,
we were told to trade our curiosity for control,
our wonder for work,
our joy for productivity.

But play was never just child's business.
It was presence.
It was power.

Play is where the mind breathes.
Where the body remembers it's allowed to move
without purpose beyond pleasure.
It's where laughter lives unguarded,
and imagination runs without fences.

To play is to remember:
I am more than what I produce.
I am allowed to enjoy this life.
I can connect without proving anything.
I can try, fall, laugh, try again.

Play softens the armor.
It restores creativity,
rekindles intimacy,
and invites freedom.

When men reclaim play,
we reclaim joy.

We model aliveness.
We show the next generation
that power doesn't always wear a straight face.

Play is not the opposite of purpose.
Sometimes, it's the path to it.

## Morning Reflection:

You were made for joy — not just duty. Play is sacred.
Laughter is medicine.

## Prompt:

- **What did I love doing as a boy that I still long for today?**

_____
_____
_____
_____
_____
_____
_____

## Mindful Minute:

Smile. Stretch. Move your body with lightness — even just your shoulders.

## Mantra:

*I give myself permission to play.*

## Evening Reflection:

- **Did I welcome play and laughter today?**

_____
_____
_____
_____
_____
_____
_____

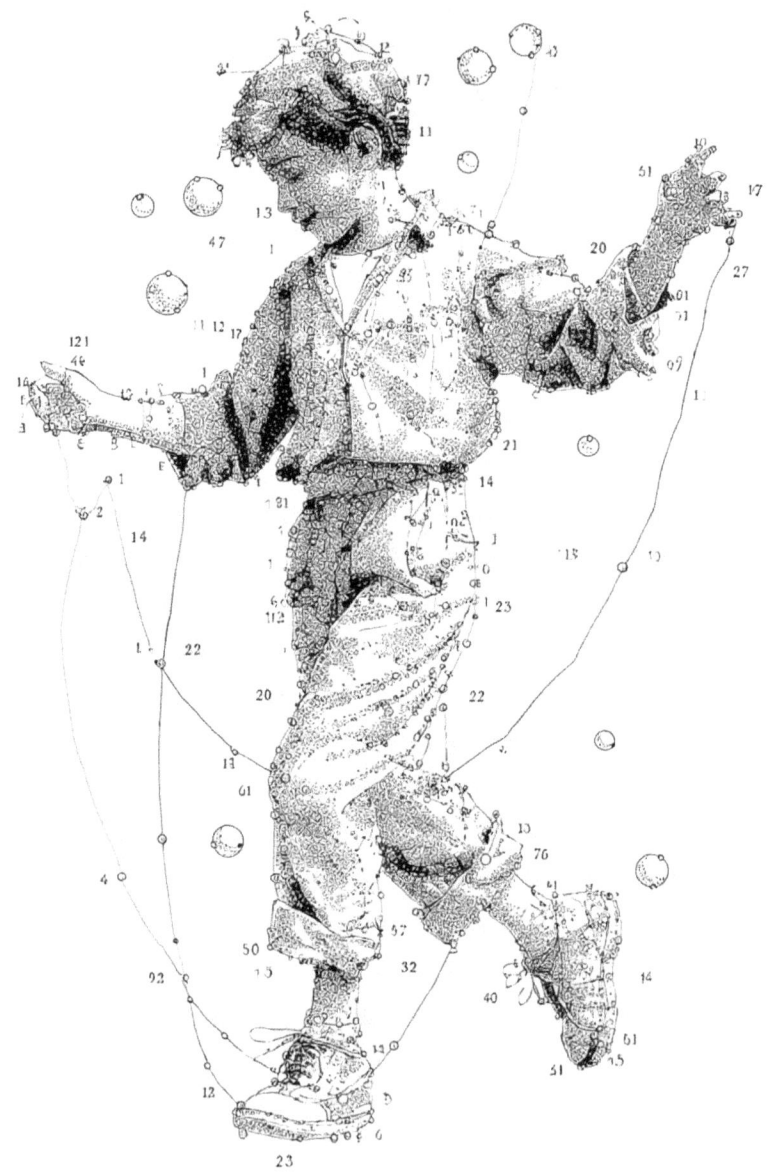

# DAY 327: The Masculine Body

The masculine body holds more than muscle and bone.
It carries stories, expectations, shame, and silence.
It has been praised for its strength,
yet often ignored when it suffers.

From a young age,
we're taught what it means to *look* like a man—
but rarely what it means to *feel* like one
inside a changing, breathing, tender body.

The masculine body is not a machine.
It breaks. It heals. It needs.
It stores trauma and remembers touch.
It desires gentleness
even when the world expects grit.

This body deserves rest.
It deserves love that's not transactional,
touch that isn't performative,
movement that's not punishment.

To be in a masculine body is not to be invulnerable.
It is to carry both fire and fatigue.
To know strength *and* softness.
To honor limits without shame.
To listen when it whispers, not just when it screams.

Today, I come home to this body—
not to fix or fight it,
but to befriend it.
This is where I live.
This is where I begin.

**Morning Reflection:**

Your body is not a machine. It's a partner. Respect it. Celebrate it.

**Prompt:**

- **How do I treat my body — like a temple or a tool?**

_____
_____
_____
_____
_____
_____
_____
_____

### Mindful Minute:

Run your hand along your arm slowly. Say: "Thank you, body."

### Mantra:

*My body deserves care, not punishment.*

### Evening Reflection:

- **Did I honor and listen to my body today?**

_____
_____
_____
_____
_____
_____
_____
_____

# DAY 328: Celebration Is Sacred

Celebration isn't just for milestones or applause.
It's a way of saying, *I see you. I honor this.*
It's sacred—because it pauses the noise
and invites joy to have the final word.

In a world that rewards grind and hustle,
celebration feels rebellious.
Especially when it's quiet.
Especially when it's for the small things—
like getting out of bed on a hard day,
saying no when it mattered,
or simply making it through.

We've been taught to delay celebration—
to wait for perfect,
to wait for permission,
to wait until we're enough.

But celebration isn't earned.
It's received.
It's how we say:
"I am worthy of joy. Now."

Today, I reclaim celebration
not as excess, but as expression.

Not as performance, but presence.
Not as ego, but as gratitude.

This breath is worth celebrating.
This growth. This moment. This me.
And that is sacred.

**Morning Reflection:**

Joy is not optional. Celebrating your wins is a spiritual act. You deserve delight.

**Prompt:**

- **What can I celebrate about myself today — big or small?**

_____
_____
_____
_____
_____
_____
_____

**Mindful Minute:**

Clap your hands gently. Feel the rhythm of praise.

**Mantra:**

*Celebration is part of my healing.*

**Evening Reflection:**

- Did I allow myself to celebrate something today?

_____
_____
_____
_____
_____
_____
_____
_____

# DAY 329 : I Am Enough

I don't have to strive to be worthy.
I don't have to achieve to belong.
I don't have to shrink, stretch, or hustle
to earn a seat at my own table.

I am enough—
not someday, not once I improve,
not if I get it all right.
Right now. As I am.

Enough doesn't mean perfect.
It means whole,
even with the cracks.
It means growing,
not to become acceptable,
but because I already am.

I am not a project to complete.
I am a person to embrace.
Soft edges, deep feelings,
mistakes and all.

Today, I lay down the need to prove.
I release the weight of comparison.
I stop auditioning for a life
that's already mine.

I remind myself:
I am enough for this moment.
Enough for love.
Enough for peace.
Enough to simply be.

## Morning Reflection:

Joyful masculinity isn't a performance. It's presence. Just being — not fixing, proving, or pushing.

**Prompt:**

- **Where am I still trying to earn worth instead of resting in it?**

_____
_____
_____
_____
_____
_____
_____
_____

**Mindful Minute:**

Inhale deeply and say: "I am enough." Exhale and repeat.

**Mantra:**

*I am enough. Always have been.*

**Evening Reflection:**

- **Where did I let go of striving and just *be* today?**

_____
_____
_____
_____
_____
_____
_____
_____

# WEEK 48 — Fathers, Fatherhood & Forgiveness

> "We are all sons. And some of us become fathers — of children, of dreams, of legacies."

This week, we honor the *father wound* and the *father gift*. Whether your father was present or absent, kind or cruel, known or unknown — he shaped part of your story. Now, it's your turn to shape the meaning. This is about healing, forgiving, honoring, and reimagining fatherhood for the man you are becoming.

# DAY 330: The Father I Needed

There is a version of fatherhood I longed for—
not always in loud protection,
but in quiet presence.
Not only in instruction,
but in tenderness.

I needed a father
who looked me in the eyes
and saw *me*,
not just his reflection or expectations.

A father who taught me
that gentleness is not weakness,
that tears are not shameful,
that emotions are not enemies.

I needed arms that didn't just correct,
but comforted.
Words that didn't just teach,
but affirmed.
A presence that didn't just guide,
but stayed.

But here's what I've come to learn:
Even when I didn't receive all I needed,
I can still become what I needed.

I can father the aching places within me.
I can re-parent my wounds
with compassion instead of critique,
with understanding instead of silence.

The father I needed
may not have always been there.
But the father I'm becoming—
for myself, for others—
is here now.
And he is enough.

**Morning Reflection:**

We all needed something from our fathers. That need was valid — even if unmet.

**Prompt:**

- **What did I most need from my father as a child?**

_____
_____
_____
_____
_____
_____
_____
_____
_____

**Mindful Minute:**

Place your hand on your chest. Say gently: "I see that boy. I honor what he needed."

**Mantra:**

*I name the need so I can heal the wound.*

**Evening Reflection:**

- How did acknowledging my father's absence or presence feel today?

_____
_____
_____
_____
_____
_____
_____

# DAY 331: Naming the Hurt

Healing begins with honesty—
not the loud kind that demands attention,
but the quiet courage
to say, *"This hurt me."*

Not everything that shaped me
was meant to.
Not every silence was peace.
Not every lesson was love.

Some things I buried
because I didn't have the words.
Others, because I was taught not to feel.
But numbness is not strength.
Avoidance is not healing.

Today, I choose to name the hurt.
To trace its roots
without shame.
To let the light in,
without needing to justify why it hurts.

Naming the pain doesn't make me weak.
It makes me real.
It gives form to what I can now hold,
understand, and release.

This is how healing begins:
Not by pretending it didn't happen,
but by gently whispering,
*"It did—and it mattered."*

**Morning Reflection:**

There is no healing without truth. Name the hurt so it can stop holding power.

**Prompt:**

- **What pain am I still carrying from my relationship with my father?**

_____
_____
_____
_____
_____
_____
_____
_____

**Mindful Minute:**

Breathe in deeply. As you exhale, whisper: "I'm allowed to grieve."

**Mantra:**

*I name the pain so I can reclaim my power.*

**Evening Reflection:**

**Did I speak or write one truth today that I've long held in?**

_____
_____
_____
_____
_____
_____
_____
_____

# DAY 332: Forgiveness Is for Me

Forgiveness is not forgetting.
It's not excusing.
It's not pretending it didn't hurt.

Forgiveness is a release—
not for *them*,
but for *me*.

It's the quiet, sacred act
of unclenching my fists
from what I've carried too long.
Not because it didn't matter,
but because *I* matter more.

It's choosing peace
over replaying the pain.
Choosing wholeness
over holding on to what broke me.

Some wounds scar,
but they don't have to stay open.
Some people may never apologize—
but my healing doesn't wait for permission.

Forgiveness is how I reclaim myself.
Not to deny the hurt,
but to stop letting it define me.

This is for my freedom.
This is for my heart.
This is for me.

**Morning Reflection:**

Forgiveness doesn't mean forgetting or excusing. It means *freeing yourself.*

**Prompt:**

- **What would forgiving my father look like for *me* — not for him?**

_____
_____
_____
_____
_____
_____
_____

**Mindful Minute:**

Breathe. Say: "I am not what was withheld from me."

**Mantra:**

*Forgiveness frees me, not him.*

**Evening Reflection:**

- **What shifted when I let go — even a little — today?**

_____
_____
_____
_____
_____
_____
_____

# DAY 333: Becoming the Father

I used to think fatherhood was about having all the answers.
Now I know—it's about being present while still asking the questions.

Becoming the father I needed
means giving what I may have never received:
gentle correction without cruelty,
discipline without distance,
love without condition.

It's learning to hold space
for small hands and big feelings.
To speak life, not just lessons.
To model apology, not just authority.

It means breaking cycles
without blaming the past—
honoring the boy I was
while showing up for the child in front of me.

It's not about perfection.
It's about presence.
It's about becoming a safe place,
not just a strong one.

Becoming the father
means becoming the man

who chooses to stay—
emotionally, mentally, fully.

For them.
And for me.

**Morning Reflection:**

Even if you never have children, you carry the *power to father* — ideas, others, and yourself.

**Prompt:**

- **How do I show up as a "father" in my life — with guidance, provision, or protection?**

_____
_____
_____
_____
_____
_____
_____
_____

**Mindful Minute:**

Hold your hands open. Say: "I have something to give."

**Mantra:**

*I father the world by being present to it.*

**Evening Reflection:**

- **Did I offer fatherly energy — to myself or someone else — today?**

_____
_____
_____
_____
_____
_____
_____

# DAY 334: Healing the Bloodline

Healing doesn't always look like grand gestures or dramatic reconciliations. Sometimes, it's as simple—and as profound—as choosing to pause before reacting, choosing to listen instead of shutting down, or choosing to speak the truth kindly when silence was the norm.

The bloodline carries more than DNA. It carries stories, beliefs, fears, habits, survival mechanisms, and unspoken grief. When I do this work—when I lean into awareness, accountability, and softness—I'm not just doing it for me. I'm doing it for those who came before me who couldn't, and for those who come after me who won't have to carry what I've laid down.

Healing the bloodline doesn't mean pretending everything was okay. It means facing what wasn't, and deciding it ends here—with me. With gentleness. With courage. With love.

**Morning Reflection:**

You may carry pain from generations. But you are also the place where it can end.

**Prompt:**

- **What generational patterns around fatherhood am I breaking?**

_____
_____
_____
_____
_____
_____
_____
_____

## Mindful Minute:

Stand tall. Breathe deeply. Say: "It ends with me. It begins with me."

## Mantra:

*I am the healing my lineage prayed for.*

## Evening Reflection:

- How did I honor the future fathers that may come after me?

_____
_____
_____
_____
_____
_____
_____

# DAY 335: If I Could Say One Thing

If I could say one thing—to the boy I was, to the man I'm becoming, to the people I love, to the world watching—it would be this:

You are not broken.

You were shaped by things you didn't choose, but you are not defined by them. You are not the mistakes you made in survival mode. You are not the silence you had to keep. You are not the anger that masked the pain. You are not weak for wanting softness, connection, or peace.

If I could say one thing, it would be this: you don't have to keep carrying it all. Let go. Breathe. Let yourself be human. Let yourself be held. Let yourself begin again.

**Morning Reflection:**

If you had one moment with your father — in the flesh or in spirit — what would you say?

**Prompt:**

- Write a letter (or a line) to your father. Be honest.

_____
_____
_____
_____
_____
_____
_____
_____
_____
_____
_____
_____
_____
_____

**Mindful Minute:**

Close your eyes. Visualize your father. Say what you've longed to say.

## Mantra:

*My truth is sacred — and it will set me free.*

## Evening Reflection:

- **How did writing or speaking to him affect my body and spirit?**

_____
_____
_____
_____
_____
_____
_____

# Month 11 Reflection: Refinement

1. **What No Longer Fits the Man I'm Becoming**

   - Think: habits, relationships, goals, mindsets.

   _____
   _____
   _____
   _____
   _____
   _____
   _____

# DAY 336: I Am Not My Father

I carry his name.
I carry his stories.
I carry the echoes of his silences,
the weight of things he never said,
and the shadow of things he did.

But I am not him.

I am allowed to grieve what I didn't receive.
I am allowed to become something new.
I am allowed to love him and still choose differently.
I am allowed to set boundaries, even with the ghosts.

Sometimes healing feels like betrayal.
But it is not betrayal to break the cycle.
It is not disloyal to become a better version of the lineage.

**Morning Reflection:**

- **You are *not* condemned to repeat what hurt you. You are not doomed to become him.**

_____
_____
_____
_____
_____
_____
_____
_____

**Prompt:**

- **Where have I feared becoming like my father?**

- **How am I different?**

### Mindful Minute:

Stand before a mirror. Look into your own eyes. Say: "I am my own man."

**Mantra:**

*I honor his story — but I write my own.*

**Evening Reflection:**

- **What choice today affirmed my growth beyond my past?**

_____
_____
_____
_____
_____
_____
_____
_____

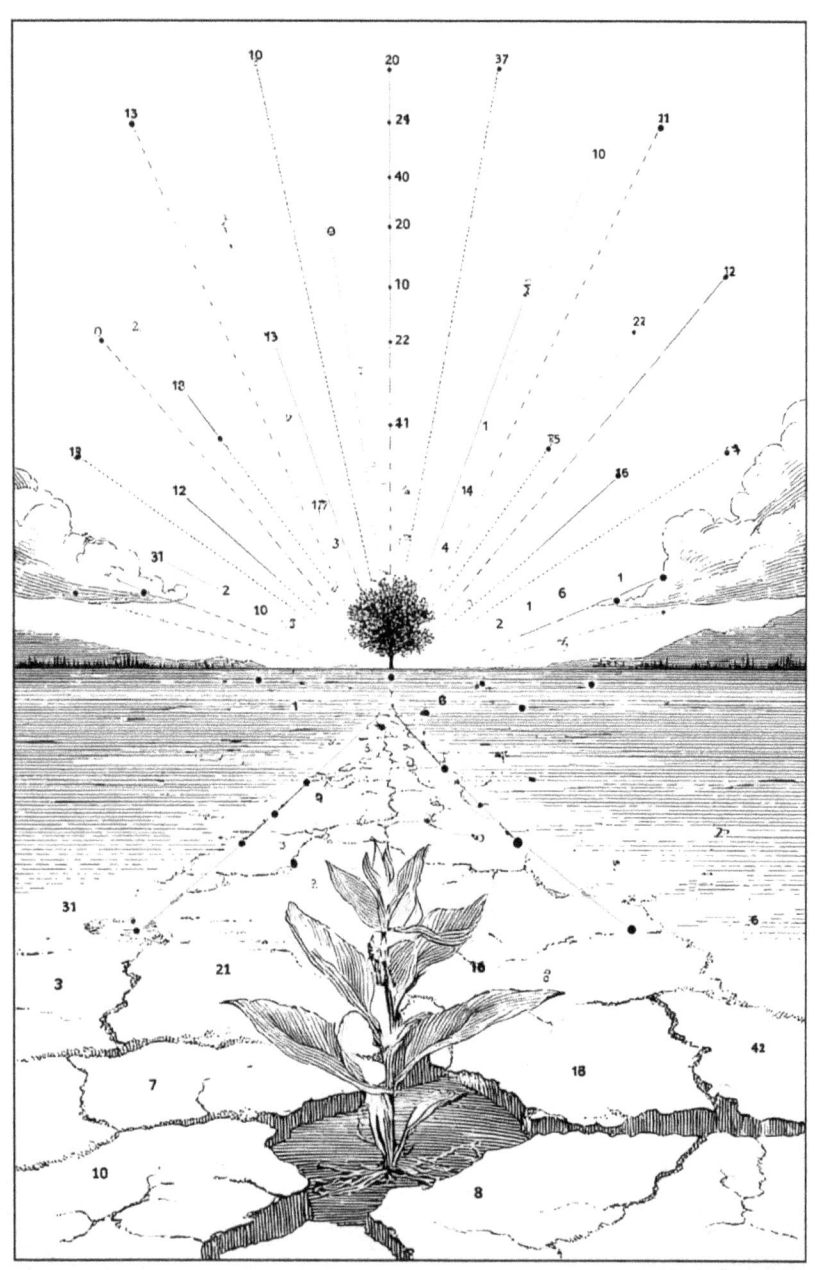

# WEEK 49 — Loved, Received

"To receive love is sometimes more courageous than to give it."

Many men have mastered *doing*. Few have mastered *receiving*. This week is about opening your heart to the love that surrounds you — from others, from life, and from within. Because no healing is complete without letting love come all the way in.

## DAY 337: The Courage to Receive

It's easy to give.
It keeps me in control.
It lets me feel needed,
admired,
safe.

But to receive?
That takes courage.

To let someone see my need,
to sit in my vulnerability
and allow love to meet me there—
without rushing to earn it,
without shrinking or deflecting—
that's brave.

Because receiving says:
"I believe I'm worthy."
Not because of what I've done,
but simply because I exist.

### Morning Reflection:

It takes deep courage to sit still and let yourself be loved —
just as you are.

**Prompt:**

- **When was the last time I truly let myself be loved without earning it?**

_____
_____
_____
_____
_____
_____
_____
_____
_____

### Mindful Minute:

Place your hand over your heart. Whisper: "It's safe to receive."

### Mantra:

*I am worthy of love — without performance*

**Evening Reflection:**

- **Where did I allow love to reach me today?**

_____
_____
_____
_____
_____
_____
_____

# DAY 338: Lowering the Armor

I built it for protection.
The armor.
The silence.
The strength that always smiles.
It got me through a lot.
And I thank it for that.

But now—
I don't want to live behind walls.

The truth is,
the weight is heavy.
It keeps out harm, yes—
but it also keeps out love.
Keeps out softness.
Keeps out breath.

Lowering the armor doesn't mean I'm exposed.
It means I'm brave enough to be real.
To be seen.
To let connection replace control.

**Today's reminder:**
The world needs more real,
not more armored.
I can lay it down—
not all at once,
but piece by piece.

And still be safe.
And still be strong.

**Morning Reflection:**

You didn't put up walls for no reason. But you don't have to live behind them forever.

**Prompt:**

- **What has made it hard for me to let people all the way in?**

_____
_____
_____
_____
_____
_____
_____

**Mindful Minute:**

Breathe out slowly and say: "The walls once protected me. I can choose openness now."

**Mantra:**

*I don't have to protect myself from love.*

**Evening Reflection:**

- **What small wall did I lower today?**

_____
_____
_____
_____
_____
_____
_____

- **How did it feel?**

  _____
  _____
  _____
  _____
  _____
  _____
  _____
  _____

# DAY 339: Letting Love Find Me

For so long, I've chased it—
trying to earn it, prove I'm worthy,
shape myself into something loveable,
as if love only comes
when I perform perfectly.

But what if love finds me
not in the polish,
but in the pauses?

What if it shows up
in the moments I'm just me—
unguarded, unfiltered,
honest in my joy,
honest in my ache?

Letting love find me
means I stop running.
It means I stop hiding.
It means I trust that love
knows what it's doing.

**Today's reminder:**
I don't have to chase it.
I just have to be here—
open, soft, willing.
Love knows where I am.

**Morning Reflection:**

Love isn't always something to chase. Sometimes, it's something to *notice*.

**Prompt:**

- **Where is love already present in my life that I haven't acknowledged?**

_____
_____
_____
_____
_____
_____
_____
_____

**Mindful Minute:**

Gently scan your day so far. Name one form of love that showed up for you.

**Mantra:**

*Love is already around me — I just have to notice.*

**Evening Reflection:**

- **Where did love find me unexpectedly today?**

_____
_____
_____
_____
_____
_____
_____
_____

# DAY 340: Love From Within

I spent years waiting for love to arrive
in someone else's voice,
in someone else's arms—
as if love was something
outside of me,
something to be earned,
something to be given.

But the quiet truth is:
I was always the source.
The well was always within.

When I speak to myself gently,
when I honor my own needs,
when I stay through my emotions
instead of fleeing from them—
that is love.

Love from within
is not loud,
but it is steady.
It doesn't need to be proven
or performed.
It simply is—
a presence I return to
when the world feels far too much.

**Today's reminder:**

The deepest love I'll ever know
is the one I choose to offer myself
again and again.

## Morning Reflection:

No external love can substitute for your own. You are your own wellspring.

**Prompt:**

- **What would it look like to love myself fully today?**

_____
_____
_____
_____
_____
_____
_____

**Mindful Minute:**

Close your eyes. Say gently: "I love you" — and mean it.

**Mantra:**

*I am my own beloved.*

**Evening Reflection:**

- How did I show myself tenderness today?

_____
_____
_____
_____
_____
_____
_____

# DAY 341: Safe to Be Loved

There was a time I didn't trust love.
I mistook protection for isolation,
and independence for strength.
I thought if I didn't need anyone,
I could never be hurt.

But the truth is—
even armor gets heavy.
Even strong walls
create lonely rooms.

I'm learning that
being loved doesn't mean
being controlled.
That being seen
doesn't mean being judged.
That receiving love
doesn't mean I'm weak.

It means I'm human.
It means I've softened
into the truth
that I am worth the risk
of being known.

**Today's reminder:**

It is safe to be loved.
Not because love guarantees no pain—
but because my heart is strong enough
to hold both tenderness and truth.

**Morning Reflection:**

It's one thing to want love. It's another to feel *safe* with it.

**Prompt:**

- **Where do I still believe love is dangerous, conditional, or fleeting?**

_____
_____
_____
_____
_____
_____
_____
_____

**Mindful Minute:**

Breathe in deeply. Say: "I am safe in love."

**Mantra:**

*I can let love stay.*

**Evening Reflection:**

- **Did I experience safety in someone's love today?**

_____
_____
_____
_____
_____
_____
_____
_____

# DAY 342: Love in Action

Love is not always loud.
It doesn't always show up with grand gestures
or poetic speeches.
Sometimes, love is quiet—
a hand on the back when words are hard to find,
a meal made without being asked,
a message that says, "I'm thinking of you."

Love in action is presence,
not performance.
It's the choice to stay when it's uncomfortable,
to listen when it's easier to speak,
to repair when it's tempting to retreat.

Love doesn't demand to be noticed.
It just asks to be lived—
in the small decisions,
the softened tone,
the consistent care.

**Today's reminder:**
Love isn't just something I feel—
it's something I *do*.
Not to prove myself,
but because showing up with love
is who I'm becoming.

**Morning Reflection:**

Receiving love means being *open* to the way it arrives —
even when it's unfamiliar.

**Prompt:**

- **What are the different ways people express love to me that I may have overlooked?**

_____
_____
_____
_____
_____
_____
_____

**Mindful Minute:**

Reflect on one person who may love you quietly. Name
their action.

**Mantra:**

*Love is not always loud — but it's always present.*

**Evening Reflection:**

- **What love did I recognize today that I had missed before?**

_____
_____
_____
_____
_____
_____
_____
_____

# DAY 343: I Let It In

There was a time I blocked it all—
compliments, comfort, care.
I smiled and nodded,
but inside, I didn't believe I deserved any of it.
I was good at giving,
terrible at receiving.
I mistook walls for boundaries,
and self-denial for humility.

But healing asks more of me.

It asks me to let it in—
the love I long for,
the kindness offered,
the peace I prayed to feel.
It asks me to believe that I am safe enough
to open the gates.

Letting it in is not weakness.
It's courage.
It's a declaration:
I am no longer available for a life
lived behind emotional fences.

**Today's reminder:**
I don't have to earn what is already mine.
I am worthy of love, joy, and softness.

And today,
I let it in.

### Morning Reflection:

You are not the man you were at the beginning of this week. You are more open now.

**Prompt:**

- **What's changed in how I feel about receiving love — from myself, from others, from life?**

_____
_____
_____
_____
_____
_____
_____

**Mindful Minute:**

Smile softly. Say: "I let love in. I let it stay."

**Mantra:**

*I am open. I am receiving. I am worthy.*

**Evening Reflection:**

- What part of me was most deeply touched by love this week?

_____
_____
_____
_____
_____
_____
_____
_____

# Week 50: The Power of Presence

As we approach the end of this journey, we return to the foundational power of being fully present. No longer lost in the past or grasping at the future, presence allows us to feel, choose, and live—right here, right now.

# Day 344: The Gift of Now

I've spent years rehearsing pain from the past
and pre-living fears from the future.
Caught in the loops of *what was*
and *what if*,
I missed the quiet miracle of *what is*.

But the present doesn't shout.
It whispers.
It waits patiently for my return.
It offers presence over performance,
breath over busyness,
being over becoming.

There is peace here—
not because everything is perfect,
but because I finally paused long enough to notice.

The sunlight through the window.
The rhythm of my breath.
The weight of my body grounded in this moment.
This is what *alive* feels like.

**Morning Reflection:**

Today is not a rehearsal. It's the real thing. What will you do with it?

**Prompt:**

- **What's one thing you would do differently today if you treated it like your only shot?**

_____
_____
_____
_____
_____
_____
_____
_____

**Mindful Minute:**

Feel your breath. Close your eyes and mentally repeat: "This moment is enough." Repeat until you believe it.

**Mantra:**

I honor the now as the only time I truly have.

**Evening Reflection:**

- **How did being mindful of today shift how you showed up?**

_____
_____
_____
_____
_____
_____
_____
_____

# Day 345: Here, Not Elsewhere

So much of my life has been lived in the elsewhere—
in the ache of what's missing,
in the hunger for more,
in the striving to arrive
at a place that always moves just out of reach.

I've chased fulfillment in future moments
and tried to rewrite the past with regret.
But life doesn't happen there.
It happens *here*—
in this breath,
this body,
this ordinary, unpolished moment.

Peace doesn't wait for perfection.
It waits for presence.
And maybe I've been enough all along—
not once I heal, achieve, or prove—
but when I decide to be *here*.

**Morning Reflection:**

Distraction robs you of the life you already have.
Attention is how you reclaim it.

**Prompt:**

- **Where do you tend to mentally escape to?**

_____
_____
_____
_____
_____
_____
_____

- **Why?**

_____
_____
_____
_____
_____
_____
_____

**Mindful Minute:**

Name 3 things you can see, 3 things you can hear, and 3 things you can touch. Anchor yourself.

## Mantra:

My presence is more valuable than my performance.

## Evening Reflection:

- **Did you catch yourself drifting today?**

_____
_____
_____
_____
_____
_____
_____

- **How did you bring yourself back?**

_____
_____
_____
_____
_____
_____
_____

# Day 346: When You Truly Listen

When you truly listen,
you offer more than your ears—
you offer presence.
Not solutions.
Not answers.
Not a tidy bow to wrap up someone's pain.

You offer space.
A sacred stillness
where the other person can unfold,
layer by layer,
without fear of interruption or repair.

True listening says,
"I'm not afraid of your truth."
It says,
"You don't have to shrink here."
It's an unspoken vow:
*I won't run from your honesty.*

When you truly listen,
you quiet the voice that wants to respond,
and amplify the heart that wants to understand.

## Morning Reflection:

Listening is an act of love. Especially to yourself.

## Prompt:

- **What have you been trying to tell yourself that you keep ignoring?**

_____
_____
_____
_____
_____
_____
_____

## Mindful Minute:

Sit in silence. Ask your body: "What do you need from me today?"

Listen gently.

**Mantra:**

I am open to the truth I hold inside.

**Evening Reflection:**

- Did you hear anything new in yourself or others today?

_____
_____
_____
_____
_____
_____
_____
_____

# Day 347: Discomfort Is a Doorway

Discomfort isn't the enemy.
It's a signal. A doorway.
An invitation to pause,
to lean in,
to notice what's asking to be healed or heard.

Most of us were taught to flee from it—
to fix it, numb it, avoid it.
But what if we sat with it instead?
What if we asked,
*"What are you trying to teach me?"*

Discomfort often guards the very parts of us
that are ready to evolve.
It shows up
when you outgrow old patterns.
It stirs
when your truth gets louder than your fear.

Yes, it's uncomfortable—
but it's also sacred.
It's how transformation begins.

**Morning Reflection:**

Discomfort isn't always danger. Sometimes, it's an invitation to grow.

**Prompt:**

- **What discomfort have you been resisting?**

_____
_____
_____
_____
_____
_____
_____

- **What if you leaned into it?**

_____
_____
_____
_____
_____
_____
_____

**Mindful Minute:**

Breathe into a memory or emotion that feels uncomfortable. Notice its edges.

Name it without judgment.

**Mantra:**

I grow through what I go through.

**Evening Reflection:**

- **How did leaning into discomfort shape your day?**

_____
_____
_____
_____
_____
_____
_____

# Day 348: Being, Not Doing

You are not your output.
You are not your productivity.
You are not a checklist or a result.

Somewhere along the way,
many of us confused our worth
with what we can prove, produce, or perform.
We learned to hustle for validation—
to be busy instead of present,
to do instead of be.

But your presence,
your breath,
your heartbeat—
they all matter
even when you're still.

*Being* is not laziness.
*Being* is not failure.
It's a return—
to self,
to essence,
to truth.

Today, choose to just be.
Sit in silence.
Breathe deeply.
Listen within.
There's a you underneath the doing—
and he is already enough.

**Morning Reflection:**

You are not your productivity. You are not a machine.

**Prompt:**

- **If doing nothing today made you more whole, would you allow it?**

_____
_____
_____
_____
_____
_____
_____
_____

### Mindful Minute:

Rest without guilt. Even just for 60 seconds.

Feel the pause nourish you.

### Mantra:

I am allowed to rest and simply be.

**Evening Reflection:**

- **What did it feel like to be instead of do today?**

_____
_____
_____
_____
_____
_____
_____
_____

# Day 349: Fully Alive

To be fully alive is not to be constantly happy.
It's to be fully *here*.
To feel the sun and not rush it.
To cry without shame.
To laugh without restraint.
To grieve and not apologize.
To hope again—even after heartbreak.

Being fully alive means letting your heart be touched.
It means embracing awe,
welcoming vulnerability,
and allowing joy and pain
to take up space without one canceling the other.

It's letting go of numbness disguised as strength.
It's choosing connection over control.
It's saying yes to the depth of the human experience,
even when it doesn't feel neat or safe.

You weren't made to survive your life—
you were made to *live* it.

**Morning Reflection:**

Feeling is a sign you're alive. Even the hard feelings.

**Prompt:**

- **What's one feeling you've been avoiding?**

- **Can you give it space today?**

**Mindful Minute:**

Visualize your emotion as a wave.

Watch it rise, crest, and fall.

Don't fight it—ride it.

**Mantra:**

*Feeling is not weakness. It is aliveness.*

**Evening Reflection:**

- **What emotion surfaced today?**

_____
_____
_____
_____
_____
_____
_____
_____

- How did you respond to it?

_____
_____
_____
_____
_____
_____
_____
_____

# Day 350: Stay with Yourself

But healing asks something braver—
**to stay.**
Stay with the discomfort.
Stay with the trembling.
Stay with the part of you that feels afraid, unsure, or unseen.
Because that part is not your enemy—
it's your invitation.

Stay when your old patterns beg you to run.
Stay when your mind starts rewriting the truth to feel safe.
Stay when it would be easier to shut down.
Because staying is how you learn to trust yourself again.

You are not too much.
You are not too broken.
You are not a burden.

You are worthy of your own presence.
You are worthy of your own patience.
You are worthy of staying—
right here, with all of you.

Let today be the day you choose not to abandon yourself.
No matter who leaves.
No matter what comes.
You stay.

With love.
With grace.
With truth.

Stay with yourself.

### Morning Reflection:

When everything gets loud, stay loyal to your inner calm.

### Prompt:

- **Where in your life do you abandon yourself for approval, ease, or escape?**

_____
_____
_____
_____
_____
_____
_____
_____

### Mindful Minute:

Place your hand on your chest and whisper, "I am here for you." Stay with that presence.

**Mantra:**

*I stay rooted in me.*

**Evening Reflection:**

- How did you show up for yourself today, even in small ways?

_____
_____
_____
_____
_____
_____
_____
_____

# Week 51: Holding Peace in the Chaos

Life will never be without noise, urgency, or friction. But in learning how to hold your peace within the storm, you become unshakable—not because chaos disappears, but because you no longer depend on its absence to feel whole.

# Day 351: Calm Is a Choice

There's a moment between what happens and how you respond.
That moment is power.
And in that moment, you can choose calm.

Not the kind of calm that ignores reality or suppresses emotion.
But the kind that breathes through it.
That whispers, "I am still here,"
even when the world spins fast and loud.

Calm doesn't mean you're unaffected.
It means you're anchored.
Rooted in presence.
Centered in truth.

You don't have to absorb the chaos around you.
You don't have to match the energy in the room.
You don't have to prove your peace to anyone.

Your calm can be quiet, still, and unseen—
but it is deeply felt.
It's the soft exhale after holding too much.
It's the steady ground beneath shaky thoughts.
It's the pause that reminds you:
you're not powerless.

Today, breathe before you react.
Notice before you respond.
Choose the tone you want to carry.
Because in a world that rushes and yells,
your calm is not just a choice—
it's a revolution.

**Morning Reflection:**

Peace isn't found—it's created in how you respond.

**Prompt:**

- What typically disrupts your inner calm?

_____
_____
_____
_____
_____
_____
_____

- How can you prepare for it today?

_____
_____
_____
_____
_____
_____
_____

**Mindful Minute:**

As you inhale, imagine calm entering your body. As you exhale, picture tension leaving.

**Mantra:**

Peace begins with me.

**Evening Reflection:**

- How did you choose calm today, even when it wasn't easy?

_____
_____
_____
_____
_____
_____
_____
_____

# Day 352: Letting It Be

Not every emotion needs a solution.
Not every thought needs to be tamed.
Not every moment needs to be controlled or reshaped.
Some things are simply asking to be... felt.

Letting it be doesn't mean giving up.
It means loosening the grip.
It means letting life move through you
without rushing to fix, explain, or escape.

You don't need to label what you're feeling today.
You don't have to make it make sense.
You're allowed to sit with the questions,
the ache, the tenderness—without forcing clarity.

Letting it be is an act of trust.
Trusting that the wave will rise,
and it will pass.
Trusting that your presence is enough.
Trusting that you can hold space for yourself,
just as you are.

So, pause.
Inhale.
Let the moment unfold,
without performance or resistance.

What if peace isn't something you achieve—
but something you allow?
Let today be soft.

Let today be slow.
Let it be.

## Morning Reflection:

Sometimes healing doesn't come from fixing—but from allowing.

**Prompt:**

- **What's one thing you've been fighting that might actually need acceptance instead?**

_____
_____
_____
_____
_____
_____
_____
_____

**Mindful Minute:**

Repeat slowly: "I allow what I cannot control. I make space for what is." Breathe into the words.

**Mantra:**

I release the need to fix everything.

**Evening Reflection:**

- What changed when you let something be today?

_____
_____
_____
_____
_____
_____
_____

# Day 353: Grounded, Not Reactive

There's a sacred space between what happens and how you respond.
That space—however small—is where your power lives.
To pause.
To breathe.
To return to yourself before the reaction takes over.

Reacting is easy.
It's what we've been conditioned to do.
To defend.
To correct.
To fix.
But being grounded asks something deeper:
presence over protection.

When you're grounded, your response comes from alignment, not adrenaline.
You become less about the storm around you
and more about the stillness within you.

This isn't about suppression.
It's about sovereignty.
You can feel the anger, the fear, the sting of words—
and still choose how you move.

You don't owe the world your emotional outbursts.
You owe yourself a safe home inside your body.

And grounding is how you build it—
moment by moment, breath by breath.

So today, before you respond,
pause.
Feel your feet.
Notice your breath.
Come back to your body.

And when you do respond,
let it come from wholeness,
not the wound.
From clarity,
not chaos.

You are allowed to feel deeply—
and still remain grounded.

**Morning Reflection:**

Reactivity is a habit. Grounding is a skill.

**Prompt:**

- What triggers you to overreact?

_____
_____
_____
_____
_____
_____
_____

- What grounding ritual could help you today?

_____
_____
_____
_____
_____
_____
_____

**Mindful Minute:**

Place both feet flat. Feel the weight of your body supported by the earth. Breathe into that security.

### Mantra:

I respond with presence, not panic.

### Evening Reflection:

- **Did you catch a moment where grounding helped you pause before reacting?**

_____
_____
_____
_____
_____
_____
_____

# Day 354: The Safe Place Within

No matter what the world demands of you—
who you're expected to be,
how strong you're told to appear,
or how quickly you're meant to move—
there's a place inside you that asks for none of it.

It's quiet there.
Still.
Unbothered by performance, perfection, or pace.

This place doesn't judge your feelings.
It doesn't rush your healing.
It holds your sorrow and your joy
with the same open arms.

It's the place you return to when everything feels too loud.
The one that reminds you:
*You are not your pain.*
*You are not your past.*
*You are not what you do for others.*

You are breath.
You are being.
You are enough—here, now, just as you are.

The safe place within doesn't need permission.
It doesn't need to be earned.

It's yours.
It's always been yours.

Today, go there.
Sit in that quiet.
Let it remind you of your worth.
Let it remind you that safety doesn't always come from the outside.
Sometimes, it's found in the simple act of being with yourself—
fully, gently, without fear.

## Morning Reflection:

Peace doesn't always come from the world around you.
Sometimes, you must carry it inside you.

**Prompt:**

- What place, memory, or image helps you feel at peace?

_____
_____
_____
_____
_____
_____
_____

- Can you visualize it right now?

_____
_____
_____
_____
_____
_____
_____

**Mindful Minute:**

Close your eyes and imagine your safe place. Let it surround you. Stay there for 60 seconds.

**Mantra:**

I carry peace within me wherever I go.

**Evening Reflection:**

- Did you find a peaceful moment today—even just a breath?

_____
_____
_____
_____
_____
_____
_____

# Day 355: Choose Not to Escalate

There's a power in the pause.
In the breath you take before you respond.
In the split-second where you *could* defend, attack, prove, or explode—
but instead, you choose presence over performance.

Escalation is easy.
It's reflex, ego, protection.
It feels like control but often leads to chaos.
It might win the moment but can lose the connection.

To de-escalate is not weakness.
It's strength under pressure.
It's choosing the bigger picture over the louder reaction.
It's remembering that not every fire needs your fuel.

You are allowed to be calm in the storm.
You are allowed to walk away without guilt.
You are allowed to protect your peace without explanation.

Today, you don't have to prove you're right.
You don't have to match the energy thrown at you.
You don't have to lose yourself to be heard.

You can be clear and grounded.
Firm and gentle.
You can set the tone, or you can choose to leave the room.

And in doing so, you reclaim your power—
not through dominance,
but through intentional presence.

That is real strength.
That is healing in action.

**Morning Reflection:**

You don't have to meet chaos with more chaos.

**Prompt:**

- **Recall a time you escalated a situation that could have been diffused. What did you learn?**

_____
_____
_____
_____
_____
_____
_____

**Mindful Minute:**

Breathe in deeply. Say silently: "I don't have to match their energy." Breathe out slowly.

**Mantra:**

I choose peace even when others don't.

**Evening Reflection:**

- **How did you hold your center during conflict today?**

_____
_____
_____
_____
_____
_____
_____
_____

# Day 356: Stillness Is Strength

Stillness is not silence.
It is not passivity or avoidance.
Stillness is presence—anchored, alert, alive.

In a world addicted to urgency,
stillness feels radical.
To pause before reacting.
To sit with discomfort instead of fleeing it.
To listen before speaking.
That is not weakness—it's mastery.

Stillness invites clarity.
It welcomes the wisdom that noise drowns out.
It allows space for emotion without being ruled by it.
It is how you feel deeply,
without being consumed.

You don't need to chase every fire.
Not every thought needs a response.
Not every feeling demands immediate action.
Sometimes, your greatest strength
is your refusal to be shaken.

Today, remember:
You are allowed to breathe before you move.
You are allowed to wait before you decide.
You are allowed to be still,
and know that you are powerful.

In your stillness,
you become the eye of the storm.
Unmoved. Unshaken.
Fully present. Fully you.

**Morning Reflection:**

Stillness doesn't mean passivity—it means clarity, poise, and power.

**Prompt:**

- **Where can you invite more stillness into your routine today?**

_____
_____
_____
_____
_____
_____
_____

## Mindful Minute:

Be still for one minute. No movement. No input. Just your breath and your body.

## Mantra:

My stillness anchors me.

## Evening Reflection:

- **What wisdom came to you in your moments of stillness today?**

_____
_____
_____
_____
_____
_____
_____

# Day 357: Harmony Over Hustle

You were not made to grind yourself into dust.
You were not born just to produce, achieve, and prove.
The world may celebrate hustle,
but your soul craves harmony.

Hustle says: "Do more, be more, never stop."
Harmony says: "Move with intention, not compulsion."

There is a rhythm to your life that feels like truth—
a pace where your body, mind, and heart align.
Not everything has to be squeezed into the same day.
Not every door has to be forced open.
Some things bloom in stillness.
Some victories come softly.

You are allowed to work from a place of rest,
to create without urgency,
to grow without rushing.

Let go of the pressure to keep up.
Let your energy guide you,
not guilt, fear, or comparison.

Today, choose harmony over hustle.
Because peace is also progress.
And you don't have to burn out
to shine.

### Morning Reflection:

Sometimes slowing down gets you farther than pushing harder.

### Prompt:

- **Where have you been hustling at the expense of your peace?**

_____
_____
_____
_____
_____
_____
_____
_____

### Mindful Minute:

Sit with your hand over your heart and repeat: "I am enough, even when I do less."

## Mantra:

I choose harmony over hustle.

## Evening Reflection:

- **Did you let yourself breathe today instead of grind?**

_____
_____
_____
_____
_____
_____
_____
_____

- **How did that feel?**

_____
_____
_____
_____
_____
_____
_____
_____

# Week 52: Becoming Whole

This final week is not an ending—it's a return. A return to the self you've been uncovering all year. Through silence, reflection, challenge, and growth, you've been walking toward your wholeness. You were never broken. You were only learning to be whole with all your pieces.

# Day 358: The Man I Am Now

I am not who I was—
and I no longer carry the shame of that evolution.

The man I am now has scars,
but they're not signs of weakness.
They're reminders of what I've walked through,
proof that I've learned, unlearned, and lived.

I've let go of needing to be unshakable.
Now, I honor my softness as much as my strength.
I've stopped chasing perfection.
Now, I value presence.

The man I am now knows how to pause.
How to breathe through the weight of expectation.
How to stand in truth even when it's quiet.
How to ask for help without apology.

I am learning to live from my center,
not from old scripts or inherited pressure.
I make room for joy, for grief, for questions.
I allow myself to be held—by others, by the moment, by love.

The man I am now is still becoming.
But he is enough.
Not someday.

Not after more healing.
Now.

**Morning Reflection:**

You've walked through 357 days of awareness. Look at you now—not perfect, but present.

**Prompt:**

- How have you changed since the beginning of this journey?

_____
_____
_____
_____
_____
_____
_____
_____

**Mindful Minute:**

Breathe in deeply. Whisper to yourself: "I've come a long way." Sit in that truth for one minute.

**Mantra:**

I honor the man I am becoming.

**Evening Reflection:**

- What surprised you most about your growth today?

_____
_____
_____
_____
_____
_____
_____

# Day 359: Lessons That Remain

Some lessons don't fade with time—
they settle deep into the soul,
etched into the quiet places of my becoming.

I've learned that silence speaks.
That presence is more healing than advice.
That not every pain needs to be explained
to be honored.

I've learned that boundaries are bridges
to healthier connection—
not walls of rejection.
That saying *no* is a full sentence.
That joy is not a luxury, but a necessity.

I've learned that I am not what I do.
That worth isn't earned through exhaustion.
That softness isn't a liability—
it's an access point to truth.

I've learned that real strength
is the courage to return to myself,
again and again,
when I feel lost.

These are the lessons that remain:
Simple, sacred, steady.

Guiding me forward,
even when the path is unclear.

**Morning Reflection:**

Not every day was easy—but every day held a lesson.

**Prompt:**

- **List three lessons you've learned through this year that you will carry with you.**

_____
_____
_____
_____
_____
_____
_____

**Mindful Minute:**

Place your hand on your chest. Breathe in gratitude. Exhale with softness.

### Mantra:

I am wiser than I was yesterday.

### Evening Reflection:

- **What lesson showed up for you again today?**

_____
_____
_____
_____
_____
_____
_____
_____

# Day 360: Wholeness Over Perfection

Perfection taught me to perform.
Wholeness teaches me to come home.

I used to think healing meant fixing,
that growth meant becoming flawless—
but now I know:
it's about embracing all of me.

The loud parts.
The quiet wounds.
The messy middles.
The sacred softness.

Wholeness doesn't ask me to erase the scars,
but to honor the story they tell.

It means showing up with cracks and kindness.
It means letting the light in *and* letting it out.

I don't need to be perfect to be present.
I just need to be real.

Today, I choose wholeness—
messy, honest, beautiful wholeness.

**Morning Reflection:**

You were never meant to be flawless—only fully human.

**Prompt:**

- **Where in your life have you been chasing perfection instead of embracing your wholeness?**

_____
_____
_____
_____
_____
_____
_____

**Mindful Minute:**

Silently repeat with your breath: "Whole. Enough. Worthy."

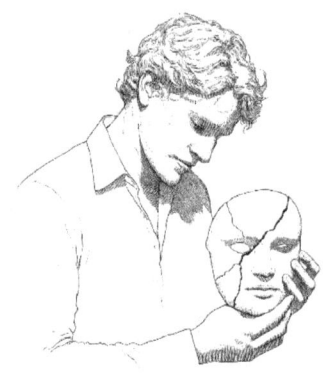

**Mantra:**

I release perfection. I choose wholeness.

**Evening Reflection:**

- **What did embracing your imperfections look like today?**

_____
_____
_____
_____
_____
_____
_____

# Day 361: Holding the Mirror

There comes a time when growth requires reflection,
not just of the world around me—
but of the world within me.

Holding the mirror is not about judgment.
It's about *seeing*—
with clarity, compassion, and courage.

The mirror doesn't lie,
but it also doesn't shame.
It reveals the stories I carry,
the masks I wear,
the wounds I've hidden,
and the truths I've outgrown.

In the mirror, I see who I've been—
and who I'm becoming.

Sometimes, I meet my pain.
Other times, I meet my strength.
Often, I meet both.

And in that meeting,
I find the grace to choose again.

Today, I hold the mirror with gentleness.
I look at myself not to fix,
but to understand.
Not to criticize,
but to reconnect.

This is what honesty looks like.
This is where transformation begins.

### Morning Reflection:

Look at yourself clearly. No distortion. No shame. Just truth and compassion.

**Prompt:**

- **What do you see in yourself now that you didn't see before?**

_____
_____
_____
_____
_____
_____
_____

**Mindful Minute:**

Gently look at yourself in the mirror. Breathe. Say your name. Say, "You've done well."

**Mantra:**

I see myself clearly, and I love what I see.

**Evening Reflection:**

- **What did the mirror show you today?**

_____
_____
_____
_____
_____
_____
_____
_____

# Day 362: It Was Always Within You

The answers you searched for—
in books, in people,
in approval and achievement—
were echoes of something deeper,
something that lived in you all along.

Your worth?
It was never up for negotiation.
Your voice?
It was never truly silent.
Your power?
It was simply waiting for your permission.

We are taught to chase, to strive,
to become *enough*
in a world that profits from our doubt.

But what if the search ends not in discovery,
but in remembrance?

The peace you longed for,
the strength you admired,
the love you craved—
they were never outside of you.

You are not missing.
You are not broken.
You are returning.

Not to who they told you to be,
but to who you already are.
To the man who can hold pain and peace,
grief and joy,
uncertainty and courage—
and still remain whole.

Today, may you stop searching for yourself
in the reflections of others.

Today, may you remember:
It was always within you.

**Morning Reflection:**

All the strength, love, peace, and power—you didn't find them. You revealed them.

**Prompt:**

- **What inner resource surprised you the most this year?**

_____
_____
_____
_____
_____
_____
_____
_____

### Mindful Minute:

Close your eyes. Picture a light at your center. Breathe into that light.

**Mantra:**

I was never missing anything.

**Evening Reflection:**

- **What inner strength did you tap into today?**

_____
_____
_____
_____
_____
_____
_____
_____

# Day 363: Preparing to Begin Again

There's something sacred about the edge—
the space between what was and what's to come.
It's not quite an ending,
not quite a beginning,
but a quiet threshold where reflection meets hope.

You've walked through fire and softness,
grief and joy,
fear and freedom.
And now, standing here,
you are not who you were when this began.

But before you rush forward—
pause.

Let the silence speak.
Let your breath return to you.
Let your story settle in your bones.

Beginning again doesn't mean forgetting.
It means integrating.
It means carrying forward the wisdom,
while loosening your grip on the weight.

This is the preparation:
Not performance,
but presence.

Not certainty,
but trust.

You do not need a map.
You are the compass.

So today, don't pressure yourself to leap.
Just breathe.
Listen.
Honor the sacred pause
before the next chapter unfolds.

You are not behind.
You are becoming.

And that… is enough.

### Morning Reflection:

Endings are disguised beginnings. Carry forward what serves you—let go of what doesn't.

**Prompt:**

- What habits, beliefs, or practices do you want to take with you beyond this journal?

_____
_____
_____
_____
_____
_____
_____
_____

**Mindful Minute:**

Inhale: "I carry what matters." Exhale: "I leave what no longer serves."

**Mantra:**

I take the best of me into what's next.

**Evening Reflection:**

- **What did you practice today that you want to keep practicing?**

_____
_____
_____
_____
_____
_____
_____
_____

# Day 364: A Letter to the Future Me

Remember the roads you've walked.
The nights you sat in silence, holding your own hand.
The mornings you rose anyway — tired, uncertain, but willing.
Each step mattered. Even the slow ones.
Especially the slow ones.

I hope you haven't forgotten how far you've come —
not just in milestones others can see,
but in the unseen ways you softened your voice,
opened your heart,
and made room for all of you to exist.

I hope you still love without armor.
That you still pause to breathe when life rushes in.
That you trust your no as much as your yes.
That you remember healing isn't a place you arrive,
but a path you keep choosing.

And if today is heavy — that's okay too.
Let it be what it is. Let *you* be who you are.
You are not behind. You are not broken.
You are still becoming. And that is enough.

With deep pride and gentleness,
— Me, from back then,
who dreamed you into being.

## Morning Reflection:

This is your moment to speak to the man you are still becoming.

## Prompt:

- **Write a short letter to the future you. What do you want him to remember?**

_____
_____
_____
_____
_____
_____
_____

## Mindful Minute:

Sit with one hand over your heart and one on your stomach. Breathe deeply. Whisper, "Keep going."

**Mantra:**

I am proud of the man I am and the man I am becoming.

**Evening Reflection:**

- **What did writing to yourself teach you today?**

_____
_____
_____
_____
_____
_____
_____
_____

# Day 365: UNHELD, UNBROKEN

There were days I longed to be held —
not just physically, but emotionally, spiritually, completely.
Days when I wanted someone to see the ache behind my strength,
to hold space for me without asking me to shrink.

But even when the world didn't offer that embrace,
even when the silence felt deafening,
I remained.
Still breathing. Still becoming.

I used to think healing required someone else's hands.
But it was my own that did the stitching.
It was my voice that whispered, *"Stay."*
My tears that softened the hardened ground.
My presence that became enough.

There is power in being unheld —
not because I didn't need comfort,
but because I learned I was never truly alone.
I held myself when no one else did.
And in doing so, I discovered I was never broken.

I am whole, not because I was untouched by pain,
but because I stayed with myself through it all.
Unheld.

Unbroken.
Unshakably, beautifully — me.

### Morning Reflection:

You made it. Through doubt, joy, grief, growth, and stillness—you stayed the course.

### Prompt:

- **What does "UNHELD" mean to you now?**

_____
_____
_____
_____
_____
_____
_____

- **What does freedom look like on you?**

_____
_____
_____
_____
_____
_____
_____
_____

### Mindful Minute:

Sit in silence. Just be. Let every breath remind you: You are alive. You are whole.

### Mantra:

*I am unheld. I am whole. I am home.*

**Evening Reflection:**

- **What truth are you leaving this journey with?**

_____
_____
_____
_____
_____
_____
_____

# Month 12 Reflection: Arrival & Becoming

1. What This Year Taught Me About Me

   - Write freely. Let it all rise—lessons, laughter, loss, love.

   _____
   _____
   _____
   _____
   _____
   _____
   _____

# Resources for Men's Mental Health & Mindful Living

Whether you are seeking help, building emotional tools, or looking to connect with others on the journey, these resources offer guidance, community, and support.

## Mental Health & Therapy for Men

- **The ManKind Project** – mankindproject.org
  A global network supporting men's emotional and personal development.
- **HeadsUpGuys** – headsupguys.org
  A mental health resource designed specifically for men.
- **Therapy for Black Men** – therapyforblackmen.org
  A space dedicated to breaking the stigma and connecting Black men to therapists.
- **BetterHelp** – betterhelp.com
  Affordable online therapy with licensed professionals.
- **Open Path Collective** – openpathcollective.org
  A nonprofit offering affordable in-person and online therapy sessions.

## Mindfulness & Meditation Tools

- **Insight Timer** – insighttimer.com
  A free app for guided meditations, sleep support, and mindfulness teachings.
- **Calm App** – calm.com
  Meditation, relaxation, and mental wellness content.
- **Headspace** – headspace.com
  Guided meditations for stress, sleep, focus, and mindful living.
- **Mindful.org** – mindful.org
  Articles, practices, and tips on mindful living.
- **10% Happier** – tenpercent.com
  A practical approach to meditation, especially for skeptics.

## Support Networks for Men

- **The Good Men Project** – goodmenproject.com
  Conversations about what it means to be a good man in today's world.
- **Men's Group** – mensgroup.com
  Online support circles and coaching for men.
- **Evryman** – evryman.com
  Resources and retreats helping men build deeper emotional connections.
- **Brotherhood Circle** – thebrotherhoodcircle.com
  A community that fosters healing and emotional safety for men.

***Books for Emotional Growth & Inner Healing***

- *Iron John* by Robert Bly
- *The Way of the Superior Man* by David Deida
- *I Don't Want to Talk About It* by Terrence Real
- *Hold On to Your Kids* by Gordon Neufeld & Gabor Maté
- *Permission to Feel* by Marc Brackett
- *The Body Keeps the Score* by Bessel van der Kolk

**Remember:** You are not broken. You are becoming. Your healing matters — to you, to your loved ones, and to the world.

# Closing Note: The Journey Continues

To the man who showed up—thank you.

For 365 days, you dared to sit with yourself. To listen. To reflect. To confront and to soften. You dared to ask questions that many never will, and to answer them honestly. That is no small thing. That is courage.

This book was never about fixing you. You were never broken. It was about remembering—remembering your strength, your tenderness, your presence, and your power. You've spent a year becoming more of who you already are. That's the real work. And you did it.

But the journey does not end here. These pages were never the destination. They were a path back home—to your mind, your body, your spirit, your wholeness. You are equipped now, not just with insight, but with rhythm. A rhythm of pausing, of noticing, of choosing.

Keep going. Not because you have something to prove, but because you know the value of being fully alive, fully awake, and fully you.

Stand tall. Walk slow. Breathe deep. And remember—wholeness was never outside of you.


With quiet strength and deep respect,

**James Broadway, PhD.**

# Acknowledgements

To every man who has carried more than he could say—
this journal is for you.

Thank you to the brothers, fathers, mentors, and friends
who model vulnerability and quiet strength.

To those who gave themselves permission to feel, heal, and
grow—your courage shaped these pages.

And to you, the reader: thank you for showing up.

www.ingramcontent.com/pod-product-compliance
Lightning Source LLC
Chambersburg PA
CBHW050254010526
44107CB00003B/316